DAUGHTERS
OF ABSENCE

"Who can return the violated honor of the self? I cannot claim that art is all powerful magic, or pure faith, but one virtue cannot be denied it: its loyalty to the individual, its devotion to his suffering and fears, and the bit of light which occasionally sparkles within him...."

Aharon Appelfeld,

Beyond Despair

"Sensitivity to separation, feelings of mourning and guilt, the desire to protect their parents and suffering people in general, are common threads running through the fabric of the lives of survivors' children. They share feelings of excessive anxiety, bereavement, over-expectation and over-protection."

Dina Wardi,

Memorial Candles

DAUGHTERS
OF ABSENCE

TRANSFORMING A LEGACY OF LOSS

Mindy Weisel, Editor

Capital Books, Inc., Sterling, Virginia

Capital Books, Inc.

P.O. Box 605

Herndon, Virginia 20172-0605

ISBN 1-892123- (alk.paper)

Library of Congress Cataloging-in-Publication Data

Daughters of absence: transforming a legacy of loss / Mindy Weisel, editor.
   p. cm.
  ISBN 1-892123-37-1
   1. Holocaust, Jewish (1939-1945)-Influence. 2. Children of Holocaust survivors- Psychology. 3. Loss (Psychology) 4. Jewish women-Biography. I. Weisel, Mindy.

   D804.3 .D373 2001
   940.53'18-dc21   2001025393

Printed in the United States of America on acid-free paper that meets the American National Standards Institute Z39-48 Standard.

First Edition

10 9 8 7 6 5 4 3 2 1

CONTENTS

"Saying Kaddish" by Madalyn Marcus

The Leaving

Gently, tenderly

disengaging

branches barely aware,

foliage in formation

creating

an array of colors—

clinging, proudly poised,

beneath lush blankets—

bountiful layers of life—

Spring's seedling, Summer's glorious gift

tended, nurtured,

defying Nature's formidable decree.

I do not wish to diminish

I long to prolong

seasons,

detain changes,

delay

the leaving

—Dassie Schreiber
    October, 1994

Acknowledgments

On behalf of all the contributors to this book, I would like to thank our outstanding publisher, Kathleen Hughes, for her great belief in this project and her tireless efforts on its behalf.

A special thank you to Noemi C. Taylor, Lisa Craig, Jeanne Hickman, Jane Graf, and all the IPM staff for their excellent assistance and devotion to this project.

To all our dear family and friends, and those lost to us, may this book always serve as a reminder of the great miracle and beauty that is life.

Grandmother Bella Deutsch

To my grandmothers,
Bella Weiszman Deutsch and Mindle Basch Deutsch
(died in Auschwitz 1944)

To the memory of my mother,
Lili Deutsch (1922-1994)

To the future of my daughters,
Carolyn, Jessica, and Ariane

Preface

MEMORIAL CANDLES: BEAUTY AS CONSOLATION

Mindy Weisel

With deepest thanks and love to Beverly Deutsch, Bervia Fishman, Phyllis Greenberger, Jill Indyle, and Ginger Pinochet for their endless supply of love and understanding. And to Nancy Sheffner, for everything.

Do we ever get used to the feelings of loss? Time supposedly heals all wounds. Does it really? Or do we take that time and take that loss and turn it into something else, something that takes the shape and the form of our loss. Is this perhaps the source of the deepest art? Is it the art that actually gives our lives meaning? There are clearly feelings that are beyond comprehension. It is these feelings that are put into the music, poetry, painting, photography, prose, and theater that enrich our lives, and that are addressed in this book. The women in *Daughters of Absence* all have one thing in common: as daughters of Holocaust survivors they have found a strong voice through their work. For these creative women, their work has been both life force and life saver.

I am one of the daughters. My parents were both survivors of Auschwitz. My parents were first cousins—their fathers were brothers. My father found my mother near death, in a hospital near the camps, nursed her back to health, and married her. I was one of the first children born in Bergen-Belsen, Germany—once a concentration camp turned into a displaced persons camp after the war. My life was about trying to be everything to my parents. Like the others in this book, I thought the only meaning my life could possibly have was to fill my parents' lives with beauty, love, hope, joy, *nachas*. I, like the others, tried desperately to erase the sadness we inherited. It couldn't be erased. I, like the others, absorbed it. I, like the others, took on the sadness as my own.

Beauty, the loss of it, is what my mother grieved for her entire life. Beauty also was the one thing that could give her momentary pleasure. Beauty in a fresh flower, a crisp winter day, a fresh cotton sheet, a bowl of cherries....

My mother, Lili Deutsch, was one of eleven children. She was raised in an elegant Hungarian home near Budapest. Her parents owned the local bakery. I was raised hearing stories about my grandmother, whom my mother magnificently, through her stories, kept very much alive for me. My grandmother, my beautiful, generous grandmother, who would feed the poor at the back door of the bakery, early in the morning, before the others got up. My beautiful grandmother who kept a beautiful home. A home that my mother tried to recreate for us in America, with her love of crystal, china, fine linens, needlepoint, and fresh flowers.

All things beautiful. I can't, to this day, pass a rosebush without stopping to inhale its fragrance—to pay tribute to my mother's love of roses.

My mother was the only one of her sisters who survived the war. She watched her sisters and her parents die in the gas chambers. I only learned, after my mother died in 1994, how she survived Auschwitz. I was always too afraid to ask, as I was too afraid of the answer. She survived, I learned, because of her rare blood type, which the Nazis experimented with, thus allowing her an extra measure of soup. This experiment and the soup were a daily occurrence for one year of her life. Her twenty-first year.

Like most survivors' daughters, while I was growing up, and even well into my twenties, I didn't know how I really felt about anything. I didn't have my "own" feelings. I knew how my parents felt. I was not allowed the normal range of emotions. If I was sad or anxious, it made them sad and anxious. And, after all, what was there for me to be sad about anyway? I had not been in Auschwitz. I did not know what it was to be cold, hungry, or devastated. All my feelings not related to Auschwitz were *naarish* (foolish). How could any feeling measure up to those one lived with after surviving the camps? So, like so many others with my background, I buried my feelings. Till I could no longer. That is when my work took on a life of its own.

The question that haunts me to this day is, how is one capable of happiness after such devastation and tragedy as my parents endured? And yet, they did know happiness. They knew the pleasure of children, of work, and a full life. But it was difficult for me to understand how one could live and be happy. How could I be "happy," knowing what my parents had endured? After what they lost and lived through?

My parents, however, insisted not only on my well-being but on my happiness. To be a good daughter was to be a happy one. Always being understanding, never complaining and always being there for them. There is nothing I wanted more than to be that good and happy daughter.

In the beginning of my life as a painter, I was, I suppose, what psychologist Dina Wardi, calls a "memorial candle." She claims in her book, *Memorial Candles: Children of the Holocaust*, that in a survivor's home, there is a child in the family who becomes the link among past, present, and future. That child grows up feeling responsible for "inter-generational continuity, the one who bears the burden for translating the emotional world of the parents into some kind of coherence."

Only in my studio, while painting, was my authentic voice disclosed to me. Alone in my studio, I was free to feel whatever I needed to feel. I could play music and dance to it while I worked, or weep deeply at life's injustices—not worrying that my tears would upset anyone. They were my tears and my joy. The desire was to put these feelings into my work. Ultimately, alone in my studio, painting became a form of prayer, a form of dance, of song, of life itself. A life that had a desire to hold onto the moment as well as to memory, to experience both past and present, and to emotions longing to be released.

Originally, the paintings were reactions to my personal history. In 1979, I completed a series of abstract, dark paintings in which I wrote my father's concentration camp number A3146 (which is tattooed on his arm), all over my work. It was the first layer of the painting. These dark paintings, with layers and layers of writing and color, were ultimately painted black, with only bits of light and color coming through.

After some years of working with this dark history and palette, and producing a large body of dark work, passionate and intense colors pushed through the black as if to have their own say. These new paintings became the "Black Gifts" series, followed by a series called "Lili in Blue." There was no black in the "Lili" series. Instead, the work exploded with the cobalt blues my mother, Lili, loved so much. I wrote her name, Lili, all over every painting I did that year. The years followed, with series of works that both responded to the world outside myself and continued to pay homage to my past. As the years have passed, the work has become more and more colorful and full of joy. In fact, after my mother, Lili, the survivor, died in 1994, the work was the most colorful yet. I took strips of fabric from my mother's beautiful dresses and did a series of paintings called "Lili Let's Dance." These handmade paper pulp paintings were my way of celebrating my mother's life. The work, in the weight of the handmade paper and the bold colors, depicted my mother's strength and love of beauty. Each piece became a thank you for life itself, and for her belief in me, her "daughter the painter."

The word, "talent," is Greek and means "responsibility." Each woman in this book has accepted the responsibility of making work that, in its authenticity, honesty, and originality, can be both felt and believed in. The women in this book have taken their personal stories and turned them into works we can all relate to. The desire to live fully; to make peace with the past; to separate from one's parents' pain, but still respect it; the desire to celebrate life, to celebrate survival, life's beauty—all these became the fuel for the works in this book. Whether in Patinka Kopec's music; Aviva Kempner's films; Miriam Morsel Nathan's poems; Lily Brett's prose; Vera Loeffler's photography; Helen Epstein's essay; Deb Filler's comedy; Kim Masters's writing; Nava Semel's fiction; Hadassah Lieberman's heartfelt record of her trip to Auschwitz; Sylvia Goldberg's writing; Rosie Weisel's diary; and Dr. Eva Fogelman's analysis—we feel the miracle of life itself. Life lived fully, deeply, meaningfully, and with the belief that there is some comfort to be found. I celebrate these women. I admire their courage and their craft and their talent. I admire the honesty of their feelings, feelings hard-earned. I admire their celebration of life in the face of our shared sad and tragic legacy. They have transformed this legacy for all time. In each of their works they have found meaning in absurdity and have dealt with feelings that were theirs only through birth.

MINDY WEISEL's art hangs in museums and institutions around the world, including the Smithsonian Institution, Hirshhorn Museum, National Museum of American Art, Israel Museum, Baltimore Museum of Art, and the U.S. Capitol. Her work has been featured in eighteen one-person shows and more than thirty group exhibitions since 1977. Ms. Weisel has been nominated for awards in the visual arts and is a participant in the U.S. State Department's Art in Embassies Program. An interview with her about her art and life aired in 1997 on CNN's *Impact*. Her work has been reviewed by the *New York Times*, the *Washington Post, USA Today, Art News*, and more. She is an adjunct professor of painting at the Corcoran College of Art and Design in Washington, D.C., where she lives. She is the author of *Touching Quiet: Reflections in Solitude* (Capital Books 2000).

Dr. Eva Fogelman, Adam Chanes, and Prof. Jerome Chanes

For Adam Emanuel Fogelman Chanes,
my creative inspiration

Introduction

TRANSFORMING
A LEGACY OF LOSS

Eva Fogelman, Ph.D.

Public representations of a private memory of growing up in the shadow of the Holocaust are the essence of Mindy Weisel's vision for *Daughters of Absence: Transforming a Legacy of Loss*. Despite the diverse creative journey of each of the women who speaks to us in these pages, an emotional link—mourning a past they never personally experienced—is present in her writing, art, film, performance, photographs, music, and creative Jewish lifestyle.

Many thinking and feeling people in the post-Holocaust generation have thought about whether they would have been able to survive the barbaric atrocities perpetrated upon the Jews in the Final Solution. But the descendants of

Holocaust survivors relate to the persecution somewhat more personally. They often question whether they would have had the stamina to survive as did their own parents, older brothers and sisters, grandparents, aunts, uncles, or cousins. Daughters of survivors compare their capacity for survival to their mothers' and grandmothers' survival. Would they instead have been counted among the murdered relatives?

This interminable grappling with a family history punctuated by outrageous losses can be emotionally debilitating or it can lead to an outpouring of creativity. Psychoanalyst George Pollock emphasized this concept by explaining that from mourning comes creativity. And, indeed, *Daughters of Absence: Transforming a Legacy of Loss* attests to the capacity of second-generation women to embrace life rather than to dwell on the anguish and torment their parents and other close relatives endured.

We in the post-Holocaust generation can derive no meaning from the Germans' senseless racist murder during the Third Reich of millions of Jewish men, women, and children, of gypsies, of Jehovah's Witnesses, of Seventh-Day Adventists, of homosexuals, of political resisters and dissidents, and of non-Jewish rescuers. And yet, if we attempt to mourn our dead family members, the ghosts we have lived with, in many cases never even having seen a picture or known a name, we ultimately face a desire to transform our feelings—grief, anger, rage, helplessness, guilt, and anguish—into a search for meaning.

It is the creative process that gives us license to speak about the dead and for the dead. Rosie Weisel writes about what she feels her murdered Jewish family would want from her: the continuity of the Jewish people and its tradition. Indeed, the spirit of her grandmothers and grandfathers, aunts, uncles, and cousins is reincarnated as she celebrates the Sabbath each week, and holidays throughout the year, with her husband and six children in Israel.

Also from Israel is award-winning writer, playwright, and art critic Nava Semel. The collection of her short stories, *A Hat of Glass*, which first appeared in 1985, alerted Israeli society to its silence about the Shoah, and its psychological consequences on the second generation of survivors. The process of mourning starts with an initial shock, and then a retreat into denial. Nava Semel's own search for details about her mother's experience exemplifies how one can break through denial. In *A Hat of Glass* the reader is privy to a child of survivors' intense need to understand her mother's ordeals, and hence, feel closer to the living and the dead.

In "Writing the Jewish Future: A Global Conversation," an international Jewish writers' conference convened by the National Foundation for Jewish Culture, Semel further explicates this feeling. She says: "The survivor wasn't a character in a black and white film, in a history book, a slogan in school. The survivor was very close, right in the kitchen where I grew up, next to the pan with the meatballs and mashed potatoes. The Holocaust survivor was my own mother."

Semel says that it is a moral imperative to remember the destruction of European Jewry, particularly in Israel. "Writing about the scar of the Holocaust is my rebellion against the rigid model of the 'neo-Israeli,' supposedly untainted by the past.... In this era of hedonism, post-Zionism, and the illusion that we can be as any other people in the world, the Holocaust is pushed once again into a ritual corner."

Whereas for Semel the familial memory that she represents through storytelling, essays, and public speaking has long been in the public domain, for other women included in this collection these essays represent a first foray into openly sharing their confrontation with the abyss. Kim Masters describes how she accompanies her parents to a small town in Czechoslovakia. On this trip, she recognizes that concrete objects, landscape, and photographs are not enough for members of the second generation to know who they are. She goes to the Jewish cemetery and is confronted with the stark reality that her lack of knowing Hebrew prevents her from finding her grandparents' gravestones.

The reader is jolted into understanding that knowing the dead and remembering the dead is singing their songs, reciting their prayers, learning their language, discussing and living the values and traditions that were important to them.

The contributors' connection to their Jewishness is diverse. Some of the women grew up in homes with a Jewish education that connected them to the pre-Holocaust Jewish life that was destroyed. These include Hadassah Lieberman, the wife of Senator Joseph Lieberman of Connecticut; poet Miriam Morsel Nathan; Rosie Weisel; and Mindy Weisel. While Helen Epstein and Aviva Kempner realized as adults that their home was devoid of rich Jewish culture, Epstein decided to attend university in Israel, Kempner celebrated her bat mitzvah, and both began celebrating the Sabbath and holidays.

Even for the second-generation women who enjoy a spirited Jewish family life, a drive persists to live between two worlds. A case in point is Miriam Morsel Nathan. Through her creative programming work at the District of Columbia Jewish Community Center, she has exposed the lives of many to Jewish culture. However, her vivacious veil is stripped away when we read her poetry, and a window into her inner core reveals "how a child of survivors can never say goodbye.... It's see you soon." Funerals, coffins, graves, grief, roll call, lovers, and dead men from another time and place are the kind of surrealistic images that live in Morsel Nathan's poetry. She travels to Germany for professional reasons to attend the Berlin International Film Festival, but she cannot avoid wrestling with the murderers of her grandparents, aunts, uncles, and cousins. The blending of two worlds is also the theme of Vera Loeffler's photography of past and present.

Another contributor, author Helen Epstein, tells us about her first trip to Germany to promote her recently published book, *Where She Came From*, which was translated into German. Like Miriam Morsel Nathan, Helen Epstein straddles two worlds. When she was a toddler, Epstein emigrated with her parents from Czechoslovakia to New York City. In her ground-breaking book, *Children of the Holocaust: Conversations with Sons and Daughters of Survivors*, we see a successful journalist searching worldwide for her peer group. Thousands of children of survivors who did not know how to verbalize the impact of the Holocaust on their lives felt validated, through Epstein's writings, for what they were feeling. Epstein's openness about her own fears of opening up an iron box, fantasies she envisioned riding a New York City train, despair about all the losses in her family and how that made her different from her peers, demonstrated to other offspring of survivors that no matter how American they become, they are living in a time tunnel—the past is superimposed on their present.

Whereas Nava Semel's writings broke through the denial about second-generation survivors in Israeli society, Helen Epstein's seminal article, "Heirs of the Holocaust," which appeared in the June 19, 1977, *New York Times Magazine* was pivotal in revealing an invisible group in the American landscape. In the process Epstein facilitated the groundwork for the creation of a second-generation movement, founded several years later under the leadership of attorney Menachem Rosensaft.

Because Epstein experienced so much of her present as if it were her ancestors' past, she decided after her mother's death in 1989 to search out the specifics by doing a family history of three generations of women in her mother's family. Through her personal search for meaning she unearths for all of us the history of Jewish women in the Austro-Hungarian Empire for the last hundred years. In her book, *Where She Came From*, Epstein gives us a case history in assimilation: the social history of Czech Jews. *Where She Came From* mourns three generations of Jewish women. By exploring their lives and the cultural context in which they lived, Epstein gives us a lost treasure that has proved meaningful not only to the second generation, but to general audiences in the Czech Republic where it has recently been published.

In "Normal," the essay for this book, Epstein is on her way from Prague to Germany for a book tour for *Where She Came*

From. We feel her fear and anger, and her sense of living between two worlds, as she crosses the border between the Czech Republic and Germany to her destination in Berlin.

Another woman who exposes a little-known segment of Jewish history is filmmaker Aviva Kempner. In her ground-breaking production, *Partisans of Vilna*, she dispels the myth of "Jews going to the slaughter like sheep." Before the commercial release of *Partisans* it was commonly assumed that the Warsaw ghetto was the only place where Jews resisted. Kempner, who was one of the first Jewish babies born in Berlin after liberation, took tremendous pride in showing her film (directed by Josh Waletzky) at the Berlin Film Festival. For Kempner, documentary film as a medium, particularly when it comes to the Shoah, is a more powerful political tool than the written word. The voices of survivors and the raw footage that accompanies their words cannot be dismissed.

Aviva Kempner's mother, Helen Ciesla Covensky, was silent about the fact that she survived disguised as a Polish Christian woman. By talking to other survivors Kempner began to understand her own mother, as well. Ciesla Covensky's abstract expressionist paintings are an affirmation of life. Thus, even in silence, Kempner felt her mother's fighting spirit. Kempner has spent her life helping other oppressed groups fight for their rights.

Another daughter of survivors who focuses her energies politically is Hadassah Lieberman. She was asked to join a U.S. congressional delegation to the fiftieth anniversary of the commemoration of the liberation of Auschwitz. (Lieberman recorded her trip in the *Congressional Record*, August 9, 1995, which is reprinted in these pages.) She has known of Auschwitz since childhood because of her mother's stories of being imprisioned there.

Writer Sylvia Goldberg prefers a more distant encounter with the murderers of her family, particularly the loss of her two sisters. During a chance visit to the Goethe House in Washington, D.C., she is given a map of Munich that spurs her to gather the details of their whereabouts, and hence, to begin to mourn.

Not all daughters of survivors who are involved in transforming their feelings into a meaningful existence are involved in politics, or education, or Jewish continuity. Some are breaking the silence by using humor. Humor is a psychological defense that we tend to shy away from when we talk about the persecution of Jews during the Holocaust. The juxtaposition of jokes and mass murder is deemed sacrilegious. But in the performances of Deb Filler and the writing of Lily Brett, we laugh with them rather than at them. The daily pain and angst of their survivor families becomes more bearable rather than overbearing when we can laugh.

Semel explains it best when she says, "The art of story-telling is also the art of healing." She continues, "Through my story-telling I embraced my mother's personal account of pain and loss, and the scar she would carry for the rest of her life. In the process I was conscious of the virtues of healing, yet I was also well aware of the fact that a complete repair—*tikkun*—wasn't possible."

Patinka Kopec, a gifted violist and founding faculty member of the Perlman Music Program, is also interested in healing. She feels that her playing the violin helped to heal the wounds of her parents' wartime experiences. She wanted to bring them joy through music.

Many dynamics come into play in the mother-daughter Holocaust-survivor relationship. Having a mother who was a Jewish victim is an added dimension in the identity and development of female offspring of survivors. Through the psychological process of identification, women tend to identify more with their mothers, though they also incorporate characteristics of their fathers. This is an unconscious process; both generations are unaware of its occurrence.

Many factors influence Holocaust survivors' daughters' identification with their mothers. Questions include: During what developmental stage did the mother experience persecution and losses? How did the mother survive? What role did the mother play in her family's survival? What losses did she incur? How did she cope with her victimization after the Holocaust? How did she communicate her experiences to her children? Did the mother experience any traumas or psychological problems before the German occupation? Who is the daughter of survivors named after?

Daughters of survivors must first appreciate their mothers and fathers as people who had a life before being persecuted. Only then can the daughters move beyond identifying as victims themselves. This is often enigmatic because when a parent is a victim, others tend to have a skewed image of that parent who is frozen in people's minds as a victim. The daughters of Holocaust survivors who have contributed essays to this volume tend to perceive their mothers as flesh-and-blood beings, rather than only as victims of the Holocaust. By recognizing her mother's positive and negative attributes, a daughter of survivors can begin to assimilate those characteristics that are life-affirming and that signify coping, rather than those elements of the mother that suggest only victimhood.

EVA FOGELMAN, Ph.D., is a social psychologist and psychotherapist in private practice in New York City. She is senior research fellow at the Graduate Center, CUNY. Dr. Fogelman is founding director of Jewish Foundation for Christian Rescuers and ADL, and co-director of the Training Program for Psychotherapy with Generations of the Holocaust and Related Traumas, Training Institute for Mental Health. She pioneered groups for this population and has done extensive work with child survivors of the Holocaust through child development research that she co-directs. She is the author of the award-winning, *Conscience and Courage: Rescuers of Jews during the Holocaust*, and writer and co-producer of the internationally acclaimed, *Breaking the Silence: The Generation after the Holocaust*. Dr. Fogelman serves as adviser to the United States Holocaust Memorial Council, and has written and spoken extensively about the psychological effects of the Holocaust.

For Franci Epstein (1920-1989)
and Kurt Epstein (1904-1975)

Chapter 1
NORMAL

Helen Epstein

In her book, Children of the Holocaust, *Helen Epstein became the first voice of the second generation. Her writings helped the world understand the difficulties faced by survivors' children. After reading her then groundbreaking—now classic—book, I found the understanding, support, and empathy I had searched for my entire life. Helen's piece, "Normal," takes us with her through the anxiety and experience of her first trip to Germany. —MW*

Are the rails smoother? Does the train move more easily along the tracks? I press my ear to the window of the dining car and gauge the sound of metal against metal. Would I be listening like this on a train crossing into Canada from the United States? Of course not. I'm traveling on a different train, the Inter-city Express. We've just left the Czech Republic and crossed into Germany.

The landscape does not change as we cross the frontier, but everything else in Germany looks more vivid, as if the people, the buildings, signs, even the trees have all been given a fresh coat of paint. The Czech crew disembarks; the German crew comes on. Is it an accident that the air conditioning begins to function? We have run consistently behind schedule in the Czech Republic; in Germany, we quickly make up the time. The Czech crew was casual; the Germans are crisp, official. Am I seeing what's there or what's in my mind?

The train is nearly empty at midweek. I'm the only diner in the dining car. The simple tables with their little lamps, white tablecloths, and silverware are far removed from the iconography of my childhood: the cattle cars with slats instead of windows, the bucket in the corner, the dogs, the endless tracks. I will be served dinner while listening to the sound of metal against metal that thousands of Jews heard during their deportation east. I unfold a cloth napkin, take a sip from my glass of ice water.

I imagine that normal travelers eat in this dining car undisturbed by thoughts of those other trains, gazing out the picture window as the countryside rolls by, noting the towns and geological landmarks they learned about at school. Before the war, my parents were among those people. My father traveled to Berlin to participate in the Olympic Games; my mother, to attend the fashion shows. When she was sixteen, she fell in love on this train with an art student who boarded in Dresden and stood with her in the corridor pointing out the sights. But I have only recently retrieved those images—my father in his thirties suit, my mother a romantic girl—and they are not nearly as powerful as the bucket, the slats, the dogs, the tracks. The Inter-city Express for Berlin departs from the same station where thousands of Czech Jews were sent for deportation during the war, Holesovice Station, about nine minutes by trolley from the center of Prague.

Now, more than fifty years later, the present slips out from under me like an escalator running backward at Holesovice Station. I took the trolley here from the center of Prague, noting the last views of the city that my parents might have taken with them: the river Vltava and its bridges; another red trolley passing by; planters overflowing with geraniums on an upper balcony. The distance by trolley from the center of Prague to Holesovice Station is so painfully short, like the distance between normal and not. "Your parents did the right thing to leave," the Czechs who would have been my friends, classmates, and lovers have told me. "You grew up normal."

I grew up in the Czech community of New York instead of the Jewish community of Prague. Everyone in it was a displaced person who had escaped Nazism and Communism and lost almost everything a human being can lose. When I was a child, the loss that seemed most obvious was people: Each of my parents was the sole survivor of his or her immediate family. Only later did I understand the importance of losing culture and language. My parents could speak fluently and be fully understood only within their own community. No matter how well they spoke English, no matter how many American friends they made, no matter how integrated into the Jewish community they became, they were not themselves in English. And, on top of that, their basic sense of self had been bifurcated by the war—into before and after. Almost all of the adults I knew as a child—Jews and Gentiles, men and women, people from Prague, Vienna, Budapest—had before and after spouses, before and after professions, incomes, relations to law, art, politics, success and failure, God.

They laughed at seemingly fixed American measures of status, such as houses, or incomes, or titles, as illusions of naïve people who had not lived through much. They valued practical skill, intelligence, the ability to improvise and adapt. Men who had been lawyers were now working as taxi drivers; celebrated members of Prague's literary world were announcers for Radio Free Europe. My father, whose family had owned a factory, now worked in a factory. My mother was one of the very lucky ones: she had been a dressmaker before the war;

she was a dressmaker after it. She was able to earn a living doing work she had chosen, not work she had settled for.

My parents had no professional agendas for their children, not for me or for my two younger brothers. They did not even venture an opinion of what work we might choose for our lives. For the first dozen years in America, they were so immersed in the day-to-day business of keeping our family afloat that they did not think much about the future. Later on, they were too tired or they had lost faith in planning or maybe they felt they could not read the culture well enough to advise us on how to compose our lives. How did I become a writer? I think now that it was my consciousness of how language empowers: my years of writing letters for my opinionated but linguistically challenged father; my years of watching my mother set out to conquer the *New York Times* Sunday crossword puzzle. I know that both my parents, *olev hashalom*, would be thrilled that I am taking the Inter-city Express to Berlin on professional business, as they did. For the third time, a book I have written has been translated into German, and I have radio, newspaper, and television interviews scheduled. In Germany, I'm a Jewish author and today in Germany, as my host will tell me dryly, *Jews are news*.

The night before I travel to Berlin, I manage to lose my train ticket somewhere in my cousin's one-bedroom apartment.

I made my trip to Germany conditional on a round-trip airline ticket to Prague, where I speak the language, drink in the views, eat the food, and have to stop myself from treating everyone I meet like a distant relative. I don't want to leave, and I spend my last hours there turning over the contents of my small suitcase again and again. How could I have lost my train ticket to Berlin? It's been twenty years since I finished psychoanalysis. My parents are both dead. I have children of my own. The war's been over since 1945. When does normal return?

What were your fantasies before coming to Germany? an intent young reporter will ask me.

I will look her straight in the eye and, fooling neither of us, will say, "I don't believe I had any."

There is an African belief that if you allow the name of one who has hurt your family into your body, it poisons your soul. All my life, I have refused to let German into my body, letting the language fall away instead of picking it up. I know I am cutting off the culture that would have been part mine under normal circumstances, had there been no war, no Nazis, no Communists. Not only Kafka and Rilke but Goethe and Heine and Schiller and Brecht. I've tried several times to learn German, but cannot properly read a line of poetry, sing a phrase of Mozart or Bach.

My mother spoke excellent German. She hired Germans in America (after she had vetted them for wartime innocence) as housekeepers and seamstresses. She even bought some German products, although she never understood why anyone would buy a Mercedes when they could buy a Jaguar. "I have no grudge against the younger generation," she used to say, "but every German my age makes me nervous. I hate to shake their hands unless I know exactly where they were and what they were doing during the war. I don't hate them. But if they disappeared off the face of the earth tomorrow, I wouldn't care one bit. It just wouldn't affect me at all."

I am riding in the dining car of the Inter-city Express, eating but not tasting the German food, tuning in the flat German landscape and tuning it out—sometimes voluntarily, sometimes not. My mechanisms of defense are so much a part of my being that I don't always recognize when they've come into play. I've always been handy in a crisis: an accident, fire, mugging. I waste no time on emotional reaction; I numb out, shut down. Now on this train to Berlin, I'm wondering why I taste nothing and have no reactions to note in my notebook. Is traveling to Germany a crisis?

What were your fantasies before coming?

I was unable to imagine coming to Berlin. Or maybe I refused to imagine. How could I imagine the encounters I will actually have in Berlin: the long taxi ride in the Mercedes, for example, with the African driver fluent in German and English, married to a German woman for twenty five years, with two children who have never seen Nigeria. He likes to chat with Americans because, he will say, Americans, unlike Germans, are curious about people unlike themselves.

The Mercedes will roll down the broad avenues laid out for tanks rather than automobiles as I wonder whether cars run more smoothly here. My driver will point out the historic sights—the Brandenburg gate and the remnant of the Berlin Wall that used to be Checkpoint Charlie—and I will open my ears but shield my heart as he tells me: "I find myself thinking about the Jews. An *auslander* is attacked here every day. I have been attacked. I have been insulted. Sometimes passengers refuse to pay. But none of what happens to me compares to what happens to the Turks. Last week they chased a Turkish man until he ran into a glass door, and, when he fell down all bloody, they trampled him nearly to death. Now the man is blind. What will happen to his family? How will they live? The police do nothing. There are protests from the Left—candle-light marches, letters to the newspapers—but always too late. The damage is done.

"I have lived here more than half my life. Each time there is another attack on a foreigner, I remember the Jews. Am I experiencing what the Jews experienced in the thirties? Am I not seeing the writing on the wall? I have a house in Nigeria. I am only waiting to see if democracy will hold. But what will my wife do in Africa? What will my children do? Then I ask myself: What will happen today? Will I have waited too long?"

The Russian taxi driver who has waited for me in his Mercedes behind the police barricades at the Jewish Community Center will tell me that Germany is the best place in the world. The smarter Russian Jewish emigrants skip Israel and come straight to Berlin. "In Israel I worked fifteen hours a day to make the same money I make here in eight. Is it normal to have to work fifteen hours a day to live? Is it normal to live in a state of war? The Germans don't like Jews. You know they wish we weren't here. But they don't shoot Jews. It's not allowed anymore. They are cold but correct."

I have had neither of these conversations yet, but after an hour in the dining car of the Inter-city Express, I decide to ignore Germany. I had wanted to measure out the territory, experience the hours, but find I am experiencing nothing but boredom. I push away my plate and take out my letter of invitation to Berlin—which, somehow, I have not bothered to reread since it first came. I notice that its directions match neither the information on my train ticket nor the minute-by-minute itinerary of the Inter-city Express.

There are four train stations in Berlin, each with its distinct time of arrival. *Ostbahnhof*, the one printed on my ticket, does not correspond to *Zoo*, my destination in the letter. A

German travel agency issued the ticket. Do they make mistakes? I recheck the stations and times of arrival. Two names, two stations. Someone made a mistake.

Did you have any fantasies?

No, I had a plan: *It will be dark when I arrive in Berlin; I will get off at the first station, run the length of the platform to see if there's someone there from the Jewish Community of Berlin, hop back on and get off at the next station. I have no German money; all the banks will be closed. If there is no one to meet me, I will go to the police, identify myself as a Jew, and say I need help.*

In other countries I am an American; in Germany I am a Jew. Jews were once numerous, now they are extinct. *Jews are news.* The police will see it in their interest to shelter me much as they would shelter a rare tiger or kangaroo. I have three minutes to get off the train at *Ostbahnhof*, run down the platform looking for a representative from the Jewish Community, then get back on the train and ride to *Zoo*. No point worrying. If there is no one to meet me, I will turn myself in.

What were your fantasies?

Okay. I am stepping up to the podium to read from my new book and I dissolve into the frame from the movie, *Nashville*, when the woman singer is shot dead by a bullet from the audience, but this time it's a neo-Nazi skinhead who has slipped in with the philo-Semites.

Or: I am stepping up to the podium, it becomes an auction block and I am open to inspection, curious people examining my eyes, my nose, my mouth, my breasts, my legs.

The Inter-city Express pulls into *Ostbahnhof*. I feel spooked by the sign, by the empty platform. I leap off the train with my suitcase on wheels and run the length of it. No one is waiting. I hop back onto the train. *I will turn myself in to the police.* I reread the itinerary. We are exactly on time.

Why have you not come to Germany before? an interviewer will ask, and I will blurt without thinking, "Why would I want to see concentration camps?"

My answer is true. It comes from the deepest part of me, the place from which I answer to my name. Of course I know that Berlin is filled with museums and parks and concert halls and interesting people like my interviewer, and I am embarrassed by my answer because not so long ago I was a reporter much like her: serious, well-prepared, professional. She is dismayed by my answer. She tells me she'd like to be normal; she'd like for Germany to be normal. But it isn't. Every time she travels, she sees the way people react when she says she's German. English people, French people, the Danes, the

Dutch, the Czechs. Sometimes she passes for English or Dutch. Do I think that to be German will ever be normal?

I let her question hang in the air between us. It will stay with me long after I leave Europe and return to the United States. What is normal? What is that state of ordinariness we both wish for? Does it—did it ever—exist? Multicultural, trans-sexual, cross-disciplinary, postmodern have exploded the idea of normal. Psychology with its dysfunctional people, families, societies have made it obsolete. When I think about it, I give up on normal. But in that place where I think of Germany as a collection of concentration camps I am startled to discover that I also believe in a normal that is defined as "not Auschwitz."

But all these conversations have not yet taken place. As the Inter-city Express pulls slowly into *Zoo*, I peer out the window. The platform is empty. On a weekday night in spring? Isn't this a metropolis? Shouldn't there be crowds? I see a short, round woman with a shawl over her shoulders and a scarf over her hair who looks like she might be a character in a story by Shalom Aleichem. Is she waiting for me? I blink a few times to check if the woman I am seeing is really there. Then I take a breath and ready my suitcase for a dignified descent from the train. I am here. I have arrived in Berlin.

Born in Prague in 1947 and raised in New York City, **HELEN EPSTEIN** is a former journalist and journalism professor and the author of five books, including *Children of the Holocaust, Music Talks, Joe Papp*, and *Where She Came From: A Daughter's Search for Her Mother's History*, recently published in Czech, Dutch, and German. She guest lectures at universities, libraries, synagogues, and churches, and is affiliated with Harvard University's Center for European Studies and Brandeis University's Hadassah International Research Institute on Jewish Women. She is married and the mother of two teenage boys.

Dedicated to
Magda Hoff Kopec
Vladamir Kopec
My parents
Jay E. Selman, M.D.
Jeremy L. Selman
Ari M. Selman
My family
My teachers
My students
Those who are not with us.

Chapter 2
MY LIFE IN MUSIC

Patinka Kopec

Patty Kopec is a master musician whose work celebrates life in its clarity and passion. Her story of becoming a musician and her attempt to fill her family's life with music will leave no reader unmoved. —MW

I cannot remember a day without music...but it was not always that way.

My love for music came from my parents. As a teacher of highly gifted violin and viola students, I feel that I am passing on a special tradition and love of music to future generations. Clearly, Hitler, war, deprivation, and re-beginning our lives three times could not stifle the music and spirit of my family.

My story begins before World War II. My mother came
from a comfortable family in Nitra, Czechoslovakia, where her
father was in the moving business. My mother studied piano,
voice, painting, and sewing as well as attending a girl's school.
Her parents had planned for her to attend the Vienna
Conservatory to study piano. However, when she was fifteen
years old the Nazis prohibited Jews from attending all schools,
so she was tutored at home and then had to go into hiding. Her
plans to pursue an advanced education in music were not to
happen. Instead, she studied practical skills, including sewing,
hatmaking, and fabric weaving. At about seventeen years of age
she had to enter a rural sanatorium to avoid deportation to the
camps, a fate that befell most of her Jewish girlfriends.

My father's family came from Simovany, Czechoslovakia,
where my grandfather managed an estate. My father was a
gypsy violinist at heart. More than once his father had to con-
fiscate his violin when he found my father serenading young
women at nearby taverns. Finally, my father realized that he
would have to take school seriously. He entered a Jesuit gymnasium, a special school that was very strict. While attending
the gymnasium, his parents, brothers, and sister moved to
America. He remained in Czechoslovakia, living with an uncle
who was a physician. His influence had a profound impact on
my father, who decided to study medicine at Charles
University. The Nazi invasion of Prague in 1938 interrupted my

father's medical studies. Because of his great concern about the future, he changed from medicine to pharmacy, which he could complete more quickly.

Early in the war my mother's only apparent means of surviving was to be married. Her sister's husband had a close friend who was my father-to-be. Music would bring them together, as they would play for themselves and others. My uncle asked my father if he would marry my mother to save her when she was seventeen years old, because single girls were among the first to be transported. In 1942 they were able to marry. My father worked as a pharmacist while he was still in school.

Despite being married, my mother still had to hide every Thursday when the roundups for transport occurred. From 1942 until 1944 they lived in Trnava, Czechoslovakia. Because my mother's father was in the moving business, he somehow was able to have the family piano sent to their apartment in Trnava. As conditions worsened, they went into hiding from August 1944 until April 1945. The nine months they were in hiding were impossible to describe. Every few weeks someone seemed to find them, so they were always running to new hiding places. Conditions were terrible, especially during the winter. They could take almost nothing with them as they moved among the nine hiding places where they stayed. For several months they lived underneath a chicken coop, coming out only briefly at night. There was no music during this time.

Prague was liberated in May 1945, ending the war for them.

After the war my father worked at a pharmacy in Bratislava, Czechoslovakia. I was born there in 1947. Shortly thereafter we moved to Prague. My mother recalled that I first spoke about music at that age. My parents often made music in the evening, my father playing the violin and my mother, the piano. I often fell asleep listening to their performances. My mother recalled that after one of these recitals, I asked, "When Daddy is not here, may I have his violin?" These early performances sparked my interest in music.

In 1949 the Communists took over Czechoslovakia, confiscating much of the pharmacy my parents had developed. Unable to live under those conditions, my father chose to emigrate. My maternal grandparents had lost all their relatives in the Holocaust. Since all my father's family had immigrated to America before the war, he wanted to join them there. However, he could not obtain visas for my mother's family. The only option was to move to Israel, where everyone was welcome.

Shortly after my second birthday, we immigrated to Israel after a brief stay in Italy. There, my father began to work in a new pharmacy. By this time Hebrew became my third language after Czechoslovakian and German. Music again became an important part of my parents' lives. My grandparents lived with us in Petach Tikvah. Since my parents could not afford a piano, my mother learned to play the accordion, on which she accompanied my father. After progressive nudging, my parents started my violin lessons when I was six years old. I soon showed talent. Being on stage came easily. Another early memory of those years in Israel was the occasional trip to Ramat Gan to hear operas, often on a school night. My parents always exposed me to music. My mother and grandmother also painted together and often included me, giving me a broader appreciation of the arts.

In Israel I vaguely remember seeing people with numbers tattooed on their arms, but my mother said that they were the result of having been in the war. I do not recall World War II or the Holocaust being discussed at home or even at school. We talked about the War of Independence and the danger from the nearby Arab countries. Everyone seemed focused on building the State of Israel.

In 1956 my father went to visit his family in America; he had not seen them for eighteen years. Shortly after returning home, the Sinai war broke out. He went to the front with his army unit. By a strange turn of fate a friend asked him to join him in a different jeep. A mine destroyed the one in which he had been riding. After the war my father vowed to leave

Israel for America because he had experienced too much war and suffering and did not want his children to face such a future.

Gathering my mother and brother, my father moved us to America, where he started over yet again when I was eleven years old. Leaving my grandparents in Israel was especially difficult for my mother. En route to America I organized musicales and a talent show for all the children on board the ship. I also performed at these events.

From bright, sunny Israel, where I had many friends and was in the top of my class, we moved to a tiny basement apartment in a gentile community. I could not understand why my mother seemed so uncomfortable in the new setting. Not only the cramped, cold, and dark surroundings, but also the absence of Jews in our neighborhood upset her. It was then that she began to talk to me about her experiences in the war and the places where she had hidden. Early on in the war, her father was slapped across the face by a German officer and lost some of his vision because of a damaged retina that could not be repaired. She felt especially vulnerable because of this episode and her own significant visual problems, including a detached retina. She also began to speak about family and friends she had lost and how she met my father.

My father spoke very little English, yet he persevered, eventually finding a job as an assistant pharmacist. To the dismay of his parents, he spent $15 of his $60 weekly salary for my violin lessons.

Living in a gentile neighborhood, my mother was very concerned about discrimination, so she warned me not to mention that I was from Israel. This seemed to cause her real fear and concern, which I could not understand at the time. Only then did I begin to ask questions about where we had come from and what had happened in Europe. I spoke no English and did not even know the alphabet when I arrived in New York. Going to school was very difficult initially. Although the teachers reached out, I had to communicate by drawing and painting pictures. However, at almost every Friday assembly I would perform on the violin. Those activities helped build my confidence and made me feel needed. Gradually I began to learn English and make friends, but I have never forgotten that initial isolation and sense of strangeness.

The first summer after arriving in New York I went to a special summer program at Mary Wood, near Tanglewood, Massachusetts. I had the opportunity to play for Richard Bergen, the former concertmaster of the Boston Symphony. He recognized my talent immediately and insisted that I apply to Juilliard. Within a year I auditioned for the pre-college program at The Juilliard School in New York, playing the Monti Czards, a wild gypsy piece, instead of the usual classical audition repertoire. Dorothy DeLay chose me to study with her. Despite my language problems, my playing revealed a spirit, talent, and intensity for music that she readily felt. Every Saturday I would travel from Queens to New York City to attend The Juilliard Preparatory Program and to study with Ms. DeLay. She became more than a teacher, and has been a mentor, guide, and close friend ever since. My mother trusted her to guide my musical career and emotional development as an American teenager. During the summers I attended Meadowmount, a special music camp in upstate New York, run by Ivan Galamian, where Ms. DeLay also taught. There I met many talented teens who were deeply committed to music. Future stars such as Pinchas Zukerman and Itzhak Perlman attended the same camp. There was an unspoken but shared feeling of having been immigrants. However, we never talked about the war or the Holocaust.

Competitions and contests were a constant part of the Juilliard experience. My parents always encouraged me to do my best. My father frequently reminded me that I could do anything that anyone else could do. He also encouraged me to persevere in difficult situations. Yet, when I didn't win, my parents were never bitter. They emphasized the importance of preparing for the competition over winning.

While my parents encouraged me in the arts, they were much less concerned about my academic performance. They seemed to have had complete faith in my ability to be successful in music. However, they did emphasize academics with my younger brother, Danny, who also went on to become an expert in cybernetics and computers, and an international chess master. This seemed to reflect an unspoken Middle European sensibility and attitude toward women.

During my adolescence my parents often made music together, my father playing the violin, harmonica, or the mandolin, while my mother sang and played the piano. They played for themselves and for family and friends whenever we were together. My recollections of childhood and adolescence center on the importance of music in our lives.

My intense desire to succeed also emanated from the need to affirm the reason for my parents' survival. Although I did enjoy performing, I truly wanted to bring joy to their lives, especially through music. Looking back, I feel my playing helped to heal the wounds of their wartime experiences. My mother has always struggled with the absence of a normal adolescence. Going from a comfortable upbringing to fighting for survival to starting over so many times has taken a toll. She gave her energy to my father, my brother, and me; however, she has had trouble moving on with her own life. Surprises and spontaneity have always been difficult for her. It was as though she constantly had to be on guard. At times I have had difficulty really understanding her fears, worries, and pessimism.

My late father, on the other hand, somehow was able to put the awful past behind him and live for the present and the future. He appreciated everything good and positive in his life. He was so proud of my brother's and my accomplishments. His optimism became my model. He believed so strongly that whatever one's abilities, be they musical, intellectual, or physical, they were yours; no one could take them from you. My father always praised me as being the best, although I knew that I was not and that I did have limitations. My parents' love and confidence in me was a great support during those formative years.

Over the fourteen years I worked and studied with Ms. DeLay, I graduated from Juilliard Prep, College, and Graduate School with my master's degree. I was her assistant at Juilliard and at the Aspen Summer Music Festival. Later I joined the faculty at Queens College in New York, where I was also the violist for the Andreas Quartet, which was in residence. Since the 1980s I have been on the faculty of New York's Manhattan School of Music.

Early on I recognized that those who loved music and supported the arts were very interesting and, often, very unusual people. These contacts broadened my outlook and served as a further stimulus to pursue my career. I made a conscious decision not to be surrounded only by musicians. The performances and summer festivals in which I participated introduced me to a wide range of interesting and special people from diverse fields, including medicine, law, architecture, media, and diplomacy. I decided that I did not want to marry a musician, although music would have to be important to my mate.

Having dated many men, it was very clear to me that Jay Selman was the right person for me. Although Jay came from Tyler, Texas, a small town, music was central to his life. Not only did he, his parents, and siblings all play musical instruments, but also his best friend, Ralph Kirshbaum, is a concert cellist from the same town. Mutual friends introduced us, knowing our love of music. Within a year we were married. Jay has always encouraged and supported me as a musician and performer. Without his support I could not have developed into the musician, teacher, and performer that I have become. He has given me the freedom I needed to continue growing and pursuing my musical career. I trust and respect his intelligence and sensitivity, and I admire his modesty for someone who is so well-rounded. He is a wonderful husband, father, and my best friend.

We have two wonderful sons, Jeremy and Ari. My late
father had a special relationship with Jeremy; however, he did
not live long enough to develop such a close bond with Ari. My
mother has had a tremendous influence on both boys. Her love,
intellect, and artistic nature have given her a special perspective
and have helped build a bridge from her generation to theirs.
Jeremy has a special love of music; Ari is a talented clarinetist.
Both have a deep aesthetic sensibility influenced by their parents and grandparents. My mother has been able to communicate the reality and the pain of her and my father's experiences
in the Holocaust without overwhelming our sons. Jeremy interviewed his grandmother for his Hebrew School class at age five.
My mother and Jeremy were interviewed for the Shoah project.
I believe her ability to share her experiences with her grandchildren has helped to heal some of her wounds.

Early in my professional career I was primarily a performer who did some teaching. After the births of Jeremy and
Ari, I decided to concentrate on teaching instead of performing. I realized that I had a special gift and ability to communicate with and inspire my students. My teaching proficiency
was the result of my having worked with truly great teachers,
especially Dorothy DeLay. To this day, almost forty years later,
she remains a close friend. My career exemplifies the special
opportunity afforded by America, where I had the freedom to
grow and to develop long-term relationships and my special

talents. This contrasts starkly with the fate of so many in my parents' generation who never knew such opportunities.

My students have come from the United States and all over the world. I feel a special empathy for those learning a new language and adjusting to a different culture. I have compassion for and a desire to help those who are in financial need. I have tried to open as many doors as possible to help them get the support they need. My experiences and observations have led me to understand the special problems of women musicians. I have tried to be a role model and mentor and to show them they can be musicians, wives, and mothers because these roles have been so fulfilling and rewarding to me. My students have become members of the finest orchestras in the world, soloists and chamber performers, teachers, and parents.

I never dreamed that I would be able to grow and develop and have the opportunity to work closely with two of the world's greatest violinists, Pinchas Zukerman and Itzhak Perlman. Since 1993 I have worked with Pinchas Zukerman at The Manhattan School in New York, in Israel, and at the National Arts Centre in Ottawa, Canada. With Itzhak Perlman and his wife, Toby, I have been a founding faculty member of the Perlman Music Program in New York for highly gifted young students from all over the world. We all share special bonds from our experiences in Israel and in America, especially at Juilliard and in the summer programs.

I have always felt that my music, in all its forms, has served to honor my parents and is a testament to their struggles and their love for me and for music. Despite the absence of a normal childhood and the terrible experiences they suffered, my parents were able to give me the love, support, and values needed to make a healthy life. My life and career have been a living testament to the presence and continuity of music and love that could be dimmed, but not extinguished, by a tyrant and circumstances. Music reflects my experiences as a child of survivors and as a parent of the next generation in America.

Since 1987 **PATINKA KOPEC** has been a member of the string faculty at the Manhattan School of Music in New York, where she teaches violin and viola in both the college and preparatory programs. She is a teaching associate with Pinchas Zukerman and program coordinator of the Pinchas Zukerman Performance Program at the Manhattan School of Music. Students come from all over the world to study with her.

In 1995 she was a co-founding faculty member of the Perlman Music Program, conceived and directed by Toby Perlman. Ms. Kopec teaches there with Itzhak Perlman, who also conducts the chamber orchestra in the program.

Hadassah Lieberman and her mother, Ella Wieder Freilich

To my beautiful mother,
Ella Wieder Freilich,
a presence in the absence

Chapter 3

JOURNEY TO THE
PLANET OF DEATH

Hadassah Lieberman

Hadassah Lieberman's mother and my mother lived in neighboring towns. They were taken on the same transport, on the same tragic night, from their family's Passover seder table directly to Auschwitz. Over fifty years later, Hadassah and I now live a few doors away from each other and are very dear friends. After reading her heartfelt record of visiting Auschwitz, I was ever more determined to do this book. —MW

It was a Thursday morning, January 19, 1995, and I was at work when the call from the White House came. Would I join the American delegation to the fiftieth anniversary of the liberation of Auschwitz? The invitation took my breath away, and in a cracked voice I responded, "If I can go...I have to go."

My first fleeting thoughts were of my schedule, job, six-year-old daughter Hana, and my husband, Joe. The delegation was leaving in just five days. Not much time to prepare for what might be the most important journey of my life.

My mother, Ella Wieder Freilich, was in Auschwitz. From childhood, I had heard her intersperse stories of that distant, horrific concentration camp with our everyday American lives. I always listened carefully, although she may have thought from my body language that I was more removed. I was always afraid she might cry too much if she continued her dark memories...and then the dreadful story would end abruptly, and we would continue the usual conversation about meals or clothes or schools. But the stories were disconnected, seemingly plucked at random from her memory, and I got the feeling there was much more there, left unsaid, in the dark, behind curtains—memories that she can't find herself.

My father, Rabbi Samuel Freilich, was headed for Auschwitz when he organized an escape of twenty men from a forced march of slave laborers. He confronted memories of the Holocaust head on, and wrote a book about it called *The Coldest Winter*. But the experience of putting the story on paper seemed to drain him of life, and he died soon after its publication.

He and my mother survived Auschwitz. Most of their relatives and friends did not.

Yet, when the call came, I had not been thinking about the upcoming anniversary. I don't spend my life contemplating these things all the time, despite (or because of?) the fact that I am the daughter of survivors. My very existence is a testimony to survival, and there has always been an undercurrent of striving to be strong and successful in my life (a trait I've seen in many children of survivors). But the specific thought of the Holocaust is not often at the front of my mind. I had never been to any of the camps, and had not planned to go. The only place I did visit was Czechoslovakia, because I wanted to go to the places where my family had lived and where I was born. I didn't have a desire to go to the places where my family was sent to die.

So the invitation took me by surprise. The mundane logistical problems associated with a major trip mixed with the painful memories, making it difficult to decide whether to go. I called my mother, who now lives in Riverdale, New York, and she was very apprehensive. She feared for my safety. Who will go with you? Who will stand with you at the ceremony? Why is it necessary for you to go?

But in the end I concluded that *she* is why it is necessary for me to go. She and my father and their relatives and friends. As I said when the call first came, I had to go.

These were my thoughts along the way:

Tuesday, January 24...

In-flight to Frankfurt

The last few days, the only preparation time I have, I cry often. I call Auschwitz survivors, friends of my mother, for words of support and connection. For the most part, they remain quiet, saying simply, "Go in peace. Bring back peace."

I am on a Delta flight and I've just finished reading some articles from the U.S. Holocaust Memorial Museum in Washington—excruciating material—describing concentration camps in the vicinity of Auschwitz and Birkeneau. I wipe the tears from my eyes, mesmerized by this world of cruelty, torture, realizing I am soon to visit this symbol of all evil.

The descriptions of the concentration camps are incomprehensible—another world, another place. The screen above me plays out O. J. Simpson's trial, Japan's earthquake. I watch the survivors from Japan and wonder, how can you not feel for these people? How can you not feel for their homelessness, their cold, their devastation...and I don't understand what happened in these camps.

I find myself looking at a picture of Joe in the *Washington Post*...sweet darling....The picture makes me feel stronger. Now Newt Gingrich is on the screen. And Chris Dodd. The world is so intrusive around me...makes it hard to come back...so I drink another glass of wine.

Before I left, my mother asked me to bring back dirt from Auschwitz. Nearly all of her family was burned and pulverized into that dirt, that stinking, evil earth...do you bring it home? Is this their grave, entire families? Where are they buried? The ovens? The crematoria? The pits? Fifty years later the stench and screams will not be there.

How evil can people be? Watch the news and you see in small snippets: Chechnya, Bosnia, the Middle East. But the sheer enormity of this evil that I am traveling to witness is incomprehensible. The enormity and the organization of it all. I know there are criminals who do ugly, horrible things every day. But the Holocaust was the product of a whole criminal society, a society of people who were educated, literate, loved music, loved art, loved literature. And look what they did with such efficiency, with so little evidence of guilt.

Wednesday, January 25...
Frankfurt, Germany, and Warsaw, Poland

A three-hour layover in the morning in Frankfurt at the new, empty airport. So empty and antiseptic it is scary to me, somehow. All the signs are in German. It is my first time in Germany, and I'm feeling guarded inside myself. I speak mostly with a woman from the State Department, telling her about my background, my mother. I pick up the newspaper, the *Frankfurter Allgemeine Zeitung*, and there is a picture of Hitler! It was taken in 1944, and he looked tired, old. It shows him viewing something with a magnifying glass. He knew then that his war was failing. But he pushed on with the Final Solution, as furiously as ever. It was in 1944 that my mother was herded to the camps. Even as the war effort was faltering, the Nazis pressed on to kill the Jews because it was an ideology to them, a mission above and beyond the war itself.

In the afternoon, we fly to Warsaw and are picked up by embassy people there and brought to the Marriott hotel, where delegates from around the world are also arriving. That evening, I go to a reception at the residence of the U.S. ambassador to Poland, Nicholas Rey, along with some of the other members of our delegation, including Miles Lerman of the United States Holocaust Memorial Council and his wife Chris, an Auschwitz survivor; Ambassador John Kordek, now with DePaul University; and Jan Nowak, director of the Polish American Congress. The head of our delegation, Nobel Peace Prize winner Elie Wiesel, and Assistant Secretary of State Richard Holbrooke are to join us the next day.

We begin to talk about the controversy surrounding the ceremony planned for Friday. Since the Communists left, the Poles have been more open about the Jews in the camps. But

Auschwitz was initially for Polish political prisoners. Poles see Auschwitz as a national shrine and museum. And it seems as though they wanted the commemoration to be more of a generic event, with no special emphasis on Jewish deaths. No reciting of the *Kaddish,* Jewish prayer for the dead. In response, some are planning an alternative service on Thursday at Birkenau. Preposterous, but true, Elie's words, "not all victims were Jews, but all Jews were victims," need to be repeated over and over again.

I am concerned about the controversy but, at the same time, I do not want to lose sight of the larger reason for our being there. I am moved to say that I understand there's controversy around us. But we should not forget how incredible it is that we're all here together, from all over the world, to commemorate something that happened fifty years ago that, at the time, nobody wanted to hear about. We need to talk about the details, but we should not lose sight of the fact that we're here as representatives of our country, bearing witness to what happened to so many people.

We decided that those of us who wanted to go to the alternative service will meet in the hotel lobby the next morning. I have mixed feelings. As a Jew and the daughter of survivors, I want to go to Birkenau. As a member of the official American delegation, I am worried that it might detract from protocol if I deviate from the schedule, which includes a ceremony at Jagiellonian University in Krakow. But everyone assures me that the American delegation will be sufficiently represented at the university.

Thursday, January 26...
Warsaw... Krakow... Birkenau... Auschwitz

We arrive in Krakow, a city untouched by bombing. Some say it is a "small Prague." Krakow: over 25 percent of its population was Jewish and 90 percent of its Jews were annihilated. Now tours are advertised to show where Spielberg filmed in the Jewish "ghetto" area. The Ariel Café is booming with Eastern European/Jewish foods and Yiddish music. The synagogue is old—dating back to the 1400s. Stone markers from Jewish cemeteries are preserved as part of the wall.

I check into the Forum Hotel in the city. Leaders from all over the world are arriving...ambassadors, presidents, kings, prime ministers. Security measures are being put into place. Metal detectors assembled. Dogs are brought in. I find real irony in the contrast: here it is, fifty years later, and all the forces of authority are being marshaled for our protection, whereas before they would have come to sweep many of us up.

All the security precautions also remind me of my mother's concerns for my safety. I don't feel threatened personally, but I begin to realize what she was talking about. I understand we have to be careful, and I know what she felt about my coming here, and how horrible it would be if something happens to me where so much had happened to her. The double-suicide bombing in Israel occurred just days before, reminding us that, for Jews, the world can still be a very dangerous place.

News of the alternative ceremony has been spreading by word of mouth, and interest in it grows. Originally planned by Jewish organizations and Israelis, it takes on a life of its own, and suddenly includes everyone; not only the American ambassador and other delegates from the American group, but every delegation from around the world decides to send representatives.

And so I go to Birkenau, fifty years after my mother left.

No one bombed the tracks. No one "knew." No one seemed to care or reach out. And now, all the nations of the world are represented as the buses travel to Birkenau. We travel with the Israeli delegation in front of us, escorted by heavy security. Elie Wiesel; Ambassador and Mrs. Rey; Jan Nowak, who tells me he will go because he must go as a Pole and a Catholic. He was one of the first to alert British leaders to the tragedy of the Holocaust during World War II.

Our bus pulls into a large parking area and we exit along with hundreds of others. We begin to walk in our own groups. I walk with Elie Wiesel, the Ambassador and his wife, and the others over the rocky, muddy ground. I am arm in arm with Sigmund Strochlitz of Birkenau and Connecticut, a friend of Elie's. He reminds me a little bit of my father.

Where are we? I look around and there are mobs of people around us walking in stone silence. We were warned about the coldness at the camps. But the weather is warm in Krakow...until we walk farther into the camps, and then the coldness begins to set in—a different kind of coldness, eerie... heavy. Suddenly, I realize we are walking near railroad tracks, and Sigmund begins to speak: "This was where the train ran into the camp. The train was able to take people straight to the end—to the crematoria." This is Birkenau, a death camp. An enormously vast space that was devoted to murder. I thought again of what my mother had told me, vague, disorganized references to gassings, chimneys, SS, *Kapos*. Her entire family exterminated...sweet nieces and nephews murdered.

My mother's house was one of the homes the Germans occupied in the 1940s. They put in phone lines and set up headquarters for the Carpathian mountain town of Rachov. They posted notices throughout the small town telling the Jewish inhabitants that they were to report to a local public school. They could take with them whatever they could carry in their hands.

They then left for the Hungarian ghetto, Mateszalka, where my mother remembered a German beating her sister on the head. They were then told to line up alphabetically to board trains to Koschow. When some of the local people saw the trains go by, they shouted, "You'll never return!" She still remembers the children's screams for food on the four-day train ride. They wanted to throw her off the train, and a woman who now lives in New Jersey asked them to "let her be, she is a beautiful young woman." Today my mother says, "Half of me doesn't want to remember so that I can remain alive."

She told me that when they came to Auschwitz, some of the Jews who worked at the trains said in Yiddish, "You are fools to have come here." She remembers how they sent her family in different directions; she was sent one way and the rest of her family went the other way. As soon as her mother realized, she sent an older sister for Ella. "Find her." And when the older sister found Ella, she joined her in the line of life and the two of them remained alive. They sheared everyone's hair…my mother remembers the screams when they were sent to a shower that they thought would be gas and there was a "mistake" and they remained alive. She remembers the piles of bodies left in their clothes, a *kapo*'s beating, the heads and the feet in the bunkers. She remembers falling deathly ill from eating soup that had human bones in the bowl.

For my mother, Auschwitz was not a final destination. She was sent to the Stuttgart vicinity to the *Wehrmacht Febrik*, where she worked as a slave laborer at night and slept during the day. When a Nazi asked her what her greatest wish was, she was surprised to hear herself answer, "sleeping one night." He put her into the office to work with other women who knew different languages. Eventually, she was liberated from a sub-camp of Dachau, and took a train back to Prague. In the days following her return, she and hundreds of others would run to the train station whenever a new train pulled in, desperately searching for family, friends, familiar faces. They were never there. And then she stopped running. For two years or more, she would go to the basement and cry until she couldn't cry anymore. She met my father in postwar Prague, and they soon married. Not long after I was born, they traveled to America, sensing—correctly—that the new Communist rulers would not be so kind to Jews.

I knew all of this—the nightmares, the casual references like, "They all died," the guilt in remaining a survivor, the questions. I think again of the soil she wanted me to bring back. "They have no graves," she told me. "It would have been better if the mothers were separated from the children so they didn't have to see them murdered in front of their eyes." I should have been prepared, no? I should have been ready. Although we never talked in any great detail about the camps, I was totally aware. I always knew about my background. I was always so aware of the Holocaust. I bear some of the hidden scars of a survivor's child. So why was I so shocked? Why? Why is the walk into Birkenau so terrifying? Let me take you with me.

First, we crowd together as delegates for the most part, others from the survivors' community. I notice a group with a banner that seemed odd. I ask Sigmund, and he tells me that this is the banner of "Mengele's children," the survivors of Mengele's experiments—his "children" and his "children's children." Then Sigmund shows me where Mengele had stood to make his selection. He shows me the women's and men's barracks. We keep walking forward. The "survivor" in me stands in awe of the kind of world my parents had lived through.

I have arrived at a different planet. This is not the moon. The moon has been explored. This is a distant planet, and those who journeyed there for the entire trip are now dead ashes near the crematoria. The others had to repress, to black out, to forget, in order to go on. This planet is one of surrealistic impressions. The smokestacks. The endless fields with numbered barracks. The latrine house with round holes for toilets in two rows, each nearly touching the next but with enough space for a sadistic *kapo* to walk down the middle and whip the women who took too long to defecate. The bunks with beds...eight or nine in each small slab. We continue to walk.

I feel the people around me, walking down this frightful road. The American ambassador to Poland had chosen to walk with us for this "unofficial" event. The American in me is yearning to believe and hope that the world will stand united against cruelty of this proportion. The Jew in me is fearful of the repetitions of history. I am the wife of a United States senator, proud to be part of the American delegation, led by Elie Wiesel, bearing witness to history.

We continue walking until we arrive at the crematoria. What can I say? I hold Sigmund's arm tightly. What can I say? I came unequipped to the planet of death, of torture, of "endless nights," as our delegation leader describes it. Everything in front of me told me you could never believe after this place. "Where was God?" I remember my father asking. "Where was God?" and he, a rabbi, believed deeply in Him. How could you ever believe again? "Faith was the cornerstone of our existence," he wrote in his memoirs. "It was inconceivable to us that a merciful father could ignore the pitiful pleas of his children. When we were delivered to the Nazis and the redemption did not occur, we fell into despair; life lost meaning.... We became an orphan people without a heavenly father."

All of these people around me walk in silence. The program takes place, people speak, people shout. *Kaddish* is said, and we think perhaps it would have been better to keep our silence—just *Kaddish* and no words. But then we sing "Hatikvah" and march back to the buses.

Auschwitz is next. A tour of one hour. I find a stone for Dad's grave. I decide not to bring the soil back with me. I had brought a plastic bag, thinking I might. But I decide not to. I will not bring soil from the planet of death. Several people tell me about the bones found in the soil fifty years later, some of them the bones of babies. If one is a believer, then the souls have ascended to heaven, and what is left should be left behind in peace. These people, the unsuspecting, the victims, the *k'doshim* (the holy) were not left behind in peace. I will not take their soil. I don't want any part of that soil.

Yet a rock endures from the beginning. It waits silently, protectively, coldly. The rock was there before and the rock is there after and the rock bears witness. This egg-shaped rock will go on my father's grave. It is small, Daddy, but it is tough, like you. It survives. And remember, in your memoirs, when you asked: "who should say the mourner's *Kaddish*?" Daddy, we said *Kaddish* as we stood at Birkenau...our voices, the young, the old, the victims, the onlookers stood together.

Elie Wiesel's friend, Pierre of France, goes with me to Auschwitz. A large, burly man, somewhat irreverent, quite cynical and sarcastic, takes me to his father's place at Auschwitz.

Block 11—the death bunker was the destination of his father who knew twelve languages and served as *schreiber* (translator) for the place. He tells me his father's story. When his Hungarian father was in Auschwitz, a young, beautiful woman was brought in. He helped her for the night. Somehow they managed to fall in love, and as she left she told him where she was from in Paris and that she would meet him in Paris after the war. When he survived he went to the address. They met and married.

Short stories, sweet, bitter, unreal. We are shown an enormous room filled with suitcases that are all labeled with the names of the people to whom they once belonged. We see piles of hair. Eyeglasses. Wooden legs. Prayer shawls. It reminds me of the United States Holocaust Memorial Museum in Washington, where similar exhibits exist. I would wonder from time to time why Washington should be the site for such a museum. What is appropriate about the nation's capital? But here in Auschwitz, I see the answer. I understand the importance of keeping evidence of the evil on display, and I also understand that there is a better chance of such a museum remaining open in Washington than in almost any other place in the world. Who knows what will happen here at Auschwitz in years to come? We already know how the Communists kept a lid on the enormity of crimes against the Jews. We do not know what the future will hold, and so it is right for us to have a museum of the Holocaust at the center of the world's oldest, greatest, strongest democracy.

Thursday night we are taken to a concert at the Slowacki Theatre in Krakow, where we hear an orchestral piece written for the occasion by a Pole. It is so jagged and jarring—deliberately created so, because it was about the camps—that I want to get out of there. I had gotten through the day and I want to run. It is so stifling. Finally it is over and we think, oh God, let's just sit down and have some life, so we go to the Ariel Café. Let me sit here and be a part of life again. Elie Wiesel is there, and I recall how often he talks about night, and we're in the land of night and we have to keep a certain part of ourselves in the night so that we don't lose it. Elie writes from the darkness, yet wants us to hope for the future, for children. Surrounded by the light and life and sights and sounds of the Ariel Café. I want to be lively and have hope, but it is too hard.

Friday, January 27...
Auschwitz

On Friday we take buses that go directly to the crematoria area at Auschwitz. I see Vaclav Havel on my bus. When we arrive, there are so many people packed together, walking forward, that it is hard to stand without being pushed. I think to myself, irreverently, that after fifty years, people are pushing to get to the *front* of the line. I think, too, that we could have been those people fifty years ago, told to undress, having our hair cut. It was people like us who walked into this camp.

I see all the world's media gathered together, pushing for position, for the best views, wanting to hear every word, and I think, "Where were you fifty years ago when you were truly needed?" How different things might have been had film been smuggled out and played on movie screens around the world!

After a few minutes, the crowd settles in. I stand near Richard Holbrooke and Jan Nowak. The program features representatives from many delegations and religions, including our own delegation leader, Elie Wiesel. I am moved when I hear the ceremony begin—after all—with the *Kaddish* and another Hebrew prayer for the dead, *El Maleh*. This is a change resulting from a meeting Elie had with Polish President Lech Walesa the day before, as was a reference to Jewish deaths in Walesa's speech.

The formal tribute begins in the increasingly colder air. A poignant moment occurs when the Boy Scouts and Girl Scouts of Poland walk around to give the people hot coffee. The elderly, in particular, reach out for cups. Watching these very young children working so charitably fifty years after the

Holocaust somehow gives us a warm feeling about the present and the future, even as it conjures up memories of all the other young children, in different kinds of uniforms, who died at this place. There was the story of the little boy who jumped off a train bound for a concentration camp with an apple in his hand. The train was at a station, and the SS caught him, took him by his legs, and bashed him against the train until he was dead. A few minutes later, one of the murderers was eating the apple. And there was the story my father told me of the parents who tossed their babies from the trains into the arms of strangers along the tracks, hoping against hope that those families would make a new home for their children.

Tears come to my eyes as I contrast the moments. An international display of solidarity, tribute, apology. Late, painful, and yet a moment of hope. Then it is over, and together we walk to our buses in the mud, past those in prison uniforms, national costumes, and, mostly, plain street clothes. All shoes and boots are covered with mud.

Friday night and Saturday, January 27 and 28... *Shabbat...* Krakow

When I learned before the trip that I had to remain in Poland for *Shabbat*, the Jewish day of rest, alone and far from my family and synagogue, I worried about what I would do. But I am not alone, and, as it turns out, staying in Krakow becomes one of the most special *Shabbats* I have ever experienced. After the marches, the ceremonies, the journey to the other planet, to stop for *Shabbat* and to share the special moment with people from all over the world gives meaning to us all. And so we sit together on Friday night with the chief rabbis of England, Poland, Ukraine, and Italy, and Jews from England, Germany, Krakow, Warsaw, Israel, America. Rabbi Avi Weiss is with us, the activist who protested the original plans for the ceremony and who has become so much of a celebrity that when the police arrested him in Poland for tearing down a sign that said, "Protect the cross against Jews and Masons," they asked to take his picture and have his autograph!

We all sing and pray together and tell stories. Of particular poignancy are the stories of the young Eastern European Jews sitting around the tables. Since the fall of Communism, they are learning of their Jewishness. Their family trees are deeply fractured by the Holocaust; many have no grandparents. Some were born to parents who were hidden with Polish Catholic families when *their* parents were sent to their death. Another learned just three years ago that he was Jewish. Perhaps some of them are descended from the babies tossed from the death trains. How ironic that Hitler's criteria for determining who was Jewish—in some instances because of quite remote ancestors—is the same relationship many of these children have to Judaism.

The next day, on our way to services, I walk behind Rabbi Weiss and see him with his prayer shawl over his jacket. People along the way, not accustomed to seeing Jews, stop and stare. Some take pictures. And I think, "Is it gaudy, is it showy, is it obnoxious for our group to be so obvious in such a place?" That is my first reaction, but then I remember Auschwitz and the hanging prayer shawls taken from the Jews who were annihilated, and now the descendants were alive and walking to the synagogue, and it seems right.

Our *Shabbat* services in the hotel are, strangely enough, joyous. We are all happy to be together, to be alive. We feel the history of the tragedy in our depths. We share our common history, common pain. We all have questions and no real answers. As we call out in prayer, rising above and beyond the evil planet of Auschwitz and Birkenau, the planet that bore witness to our people's destruction, we all turn to the very God that had not answered the prayers of our parents and their parents as the crematoria burned their bodies into ashes.

Nothing on that planet gives you faith, hope, answers. Nothing there gives you hope for mankind. And yet, as I walked with my fellow travelers that day, as I felt their bodies near me, heard their feet in the mud and stones, walking silently, I knew our walk was prayer. Our walk might defy—bear witness. Our walk might challenge any evils as great, as powerful, as wicked and so, on Friday night we all felt history around us. We were defying Hitler and his henchmen. I thought back to 1988, when I joined my husband on his first visit to the historic chamber of the Senate, where the historian lectured us about the famous figures in American history who had occupied these seats. I had looked at Joe and asked him what he was thinking, and he talked about how proud and honored he was to be part of this rich history. "What about you? What are you thinking?" he asked. "About Hitler," I replied. "About how he tried to annihilate all the Jews, and here I am on the floor of the Senate, the wife of a senator. I am thinking about throwing my fist up in the air in defiance to Hitler."

That is the feeling I had again, more powerfully than ever before, at Birkenau and Auschwitz. We were rising above the defiled and tortured and abandoned. We were free Jews singing to God, responsible for one another.

Am yisrael chai. The people of Israel live. The Israeli flag was around us and we knew how great was our need for a place of refuge, wanting to trust, but learning the bitter lessons of history. We Americans felt how special our country is, a country where a Jew could become a senator, and where his wife, a child of survivors, could be chosen by the president to participate in the commemoration of the liberation—the destruction—of the planet of death.

I had to go. No matter how much you read and how much you hear about it and how much you talk to your family and parents—even if you are as close to the Holocaust as the child of survivors—you have to go there and see this horrendously evil, evil, evil place that stinks in its profanity, that is so ugly it shakes your belief in everything, your belief in mankind and your faith in God. And you won't understand. But you will *know.*

Now, home with my family, I look forward to the day when I travel to the grave of my father in New Jersey and place the stone from Auschwitz on the ground that contains his remains, confident that his spirit survives in eternity, never again to live on a planet of death. Never again.

HADASSAH FREILICH LIEBERMAN was born in Prague, Czechoslovakia, in 1948 to Rabbi Samuel and Ella Freilich. Both of her parents are holocaust survivors, her mother of Auschwitz and her father of a Nazi slave labor camp. Her family immigrated to the United States in 1949 and settled in Garner, Massachusetts. Mrs. Lieberman graduated from Boston University in 1970 with a bachelor's degree in government and dramatics. She received a master's degree the following year from Northeastern University in international relations and American government.

Mrs. Lieberman's professional work has been in the area of health care. More recently she has dedicated her efforts to women's health care issues, particularly promoting awareness and prevention of heart disease. She serves on the Board of Directors of Best Friends, a youth development and character building program for teenage girls; Meridian House, a non profit educational institution that promotes international understanding; and the Auschwitz Jewish Center Foundation, which memorializes victims of the Holocaust.

Hadassah is married to Senator Joe Lieberman of Connecticut; they have four children, Matt who is married to April, Rebecca, Ethan who is married to Ariela Migdal, Hana and two grandchildren.

Sidonia and Salamou Eberstark in about 1940

To Nicholas Winton,
organizer of the Kindertransport,
and the courage of the families who
entrusted their little ones to him.

Chapter 4
IT ISN'T EASY BEING HAPPY

Kim Masters

Kim Masters is one of my favorite contemporary journalists. I was delighted when she agreed to write a piece for this book about her trip with her parents to their hometowns in Czechoslovakia. From the first sentence to the last I wept. She writes from the heart. —MW

The first time my mother passed through Prague she had just turned fourteen and she didn't get off the train. It was 1939, and the breath of the Nazis was so hot on my grandparents' necks that they had put their children on a children's refugee transport out of the country, flinging their three young daughters to the uncertain mercies of strangers in a faraway foreign country.

What dubious comfort the *Kindertransport* must have provided. The oldest girl was not quite sixteen—just old enough to make the cut. The little one was ten—so much the baby that my grandmother put her on the train, pulled her off the train, and put her on again, finally relinquishing her to an unknown that seemed safer than whatever lay ahead in Czechoslovakia. The unimaginable horror.

The three dark-eyed girls wore identification numbers on boards hung around their necks. They were bound for England, destined for a children's home in the country. Strangers had signed for each of them, guaranteeing that they would not become young burdens on the state. For a time, my mother received letters from home, including a desperately optimistic one at Passover. The last one was dated March 1942.

As I grew up in America, my mother's village of Trstena seemed like some Eastern European version of Brigadoon: a mythical place that had vanished into the mists of the Tatra mountains. It simply eluded me that the town still existed in some form. My grandparents were phantasms to me. My mother, who never got a chance to see them through the angry eyes of adolescence, could only describe them in childlike terms. In her hagiography, my grandmother was an utterly self-less woman who struggled to make a few coins buy the groceries each day. When all the family took turns bathing in a tub in the kitchen, she would go last, immersing herself in the grimy water. In one early photo she looks astonishingly pretty. The last pictures show a somewhat pot-bellied matron in a matronly white-collared dress. She was forty-four—a year younger than I am now.

My grandfather was even more shadowy to me. In the few photographs that survive, he seemed to be almost a Chaplinesque figure, with his little mustache and his dapper hat. But my mother described him as a stern figure who demanded strict religious observance. Once, there was an exotic treat in the village: a film was shown on a Friday evening. It was the Sabbath, but somehow the girls got special permission to go. Then there was a power failure and the children started romping and shouting in the dark. In a terrifying moment, my grandfather appeared in the doorway, furious that his children were making such a display on a night that should have been devoted to prayer. That is the only story that I know about the bald man in the sepia-toned pictures.

My grandparents' fate was sketchy to me for many years. They had died in a concentration camp, we were told. I didn't know what a concentration camp was, and for many years I never asked. I knew it was a place from which they had never emerged, but I also assumed, with a child's logic, that any place described as a camp might not be entirely bad.

Years later, long after I had learned just how sadly wrong my assumptions had been, we suddenly decided to visit Trstena. It struck me with a strange force that this was something we could actually do. I was to fly in from Los Angeles; my parents made the trip from Washington, D.C. We met in Prague and embarked on a long train ride.

The fabled Trstena of my mother's youth was a green, beautiful place where children gathered tiny, perfumed strawberries growing wild in the deep woods. I never imagined that there was winter there at all. Now, as we drew near, I couldn't picture the real Trstena at all. We rode on the train for mile after mile, passing fields of brilliant yellow flowers. It almost seemed that you couldn't get to Trstena after all. Hours passed, and we had hours yet to travel.

We got off the train stiff-legged in Zilina, a town my grandparents had passed through on their way to Auschwitz. We thought we would be able to rent a car there. The Slovak government had offered a brochure promising half-a-dozen agencies. But Zilina was a run-down, seamy-looking place. And we were warned by a surprised but friendly stranger who helped us drag our luggage up the steep steps of the train station that we wouldn't find any cars for rent here.

Finally we hired a cab driver to take us on the two-hour trip to Trstena and help us find a hotel there. The countryside became rugged; steep hills covered with fir trees rolled past. It was beautiful country, dotted with little houses made of stucco or logs. Stout old ladies trudged along the road wearing head kerchiefs and long, dark skirts. In the fields, one or two people worked the land by hand. Every now and again, we passed a village with a gray, communist-era housing project planted near the town square. We passed one such place, Dolny Kubin, where my mother had taken a long train ride every day to attend an advanced high school. Until the advent of the Nazis. After that, her parents didn't send her there any more. She sat glumly in classes at the vocational school in her home village.

It isn't easy to be happy if you're a Jew. Perhaps it isn't easy, either, if you're from Cambodia or South Africa or Guatemala, but it certainly isn't easy if you're a Jew. It seems a dangerous proposition. Still, it was hard not to feel a bit giddy as we returned to Trstena. And I did feel that I was returning, though I had never been there before. When we finally saw a sign marking our arrival in the town, I was so excited I jumped out of the cab to have my picture taken.

And what did we find? Another village, with a main square, a couple of churches, rows of little shops along the street. But this was our village. My grandfather played cards there in that rather ornate coffee house—just an empty storefront now, with frosted-glass signs promising *pivo* (beer) and *teple jedla* (warm meals) still visible in the streaked windows.

The Soviets had been busy here, and the outlines of the original village were a little blurred by an ugly, looming apartment building. But Trstena was still just a collection of a few streets in either direction. Not a place where one could get lost, even now.

We went straightaway to the spot that we most wanted to see—the house that my grandfather had built with his own hands. A beige stucco structure on a corner, just as it was in the brown photos. It had been new when my mother left for good; now it stood, more than fifty years later, dilapidated but occupied. I knocked—boldly, I hoped—but no one was home. A low wall stood in front with a strand of barbed wire hung across. My mother was shocked by the house's condition, but I was amazed to find it still there, however forlorn it looked.

The backyard was chockablock with bricks and lumber and building materials. I had seen pictures from the time when there was a small barn there—a photo of my grandmother standing on the spot where I now stood, posing beside the family's cow.

Across the street was the play yard of the elementary school where a maid used to bring the pan of eggs that my mother hadn't eaten at breakfast. A few doors away, the pharmacy where my mother fetched leeches for her grandmother. Nearby, the little two-story synagogue, now a blank-faced, empty structure with tablets on the façade scrubbed clean of their Hebrew letters.

I took pictures of everything—the house, the synagogue, the school, the pharmacy—attracting stares from the villagers. Were we imagining things or did they know who we were? Their gazes made us uncomfortable, but we were determined to ignore them. This was our place, after all. Some of these very people, I supposed, had helped themselves to my grandmother's linen and cookware and finally to the house itself. Were we the intruders?

If so, I still felt a sense of triumph, even as I recognized how absolutely powerless we would have been had we simply stood on that spot a few decades earlier. We were tourists now, prosperous tourists, and we hadn't died. We weren't exterminated, after all. We had returned to look down our American noses at the gray post-Soviet squalor of this run-down little village.

The cemetery was almost invisible from the road, up a steep hill just outside the town. The cab driver was baffled. What we would want with this place? This is a Jewish cemetery, he told us in a confidential tone. We nodded and set off to climb the wet, grassy hill.

Behind a broken wall, we found the overgrown grave-stones. Most were engraved in Hebrew, which we couldn't read. None was dated later than 1942. Many were smashed or toppled; the good citizens of Trstena had tried to murder even the ghosts, it seems.

Somewhere there was my great-grandmother's grave. My mother remembered how her own mother prostrated herself with grief on the spot. But we couldn't find the stone. What would my stern grandfather have thought of that? His American grandchildren had never learned Hebrew, didn't observe the Sabbath—some of us had even married outside the faith. In the cemetery, there was only the chirping of birds.

Back in Trstena, we found just one hotel, and when we took a closer look it seemed to be a brothel, too. There were brightly colored condoms for sale at the cash register, and gilt-framed drawings of couples in romantic embraces graced the bedroom walls. We would not be sleeping in Trstena that night.

When it was all over, there were still no answers to many of my questions. Who were we? Who had we been? What did we become because of Hitler, and what in spite of him?

I still didn't know my grandparents at all. There was never an inch of film to bring them to life in my imagination.

The few flat photographs and my mother's childlike recollections weren't nearly enough. I had only a taste of the faraway world in which they lived, and I felt the wonder that anyone got out of there at all.

Did they take comfort in having saved their children— did they even suspect that they had succeeded before their grim journey came to an end? Or did they despair that they had brought new life into the world?

It isn't easy to be happy if you're a Jew. As you float along on your happiness, the fingertips of the six million brush you from beneath, like kelp reaching up from the bottom of the sea. You can hear their whispers. Some say, "Remember!" Others say, "Beware!" But some, perhaps including my grandparents, say, "Go with God."

And sometimes, I think, some might even say, "Thank you for living."

KIM MASTERS is the daughter of Alice Masters, who left Slovakia on the *Kindertransport*, and Peter Masters, who escaped from Vienna as a youth and chronicled his wartime service in a secret British commando unit in his book, *Striking Back*. Kim Masters is a contributing editor for *Vanity Fair* magazine and a correspondent covering the entertainment industry for Inside.com. A former reporter for the *Washington Post* and *Time* magazine, Masters has written two books, *The Keys to the Kingdom: How Michael Eisner Lost His Grip* and *Hit & Run: How Jon Peters and Peter Guber Took Sony for a Ride in Hollywood*. She lives in Los Angeles with her husband and daughter.

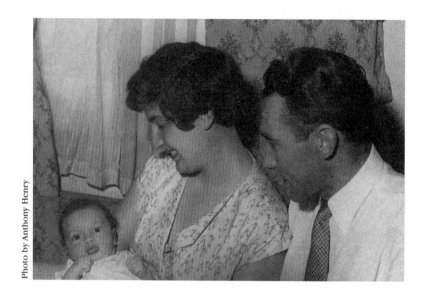

To my loving mother, Ruth,
survivor of a survivor

Chapter 5

KICKING AND WEEPING

Deb Filler

Deb Filler, a great comedian and playwright, uses her humor to master tragedy. No one else has the power to make me laugh and cry at the same time. —MW

Usually when people hear I was born in New Zealand they ask, "Reeeeeally? There are Jews in Noo Zeeealand?"

There aren't a lot of us: my mother, my sister, and my cousin Lenny. There were twelve tribes of Israel, and they wandered.

Noo Zeeealand. Third island on your right, past the Wendy's. Can't miss it. If you drive past a pink house with a palm tree and a Caddy in the drive, you've gone too far. You're in Florida.

And God said, "Send a tribe to 'Noo Zeeland'!

No, I've changed my mind. Send two people.

And they shall be known as Ruthie and Solly

and their tribe shall be known as Ki-brews,

Kiwi Hebrews."

New York, 1990

I was living and studying in the Village. The Lower East Side is very different from New Zealand. There are a lot more Jews. My apartment was in a building where hundreds of immigrants before me had made their homes, directly above The Cauldron, a kosher-macrobiotic restaurant where Allen Ginsberg and his friends ate. Each week I bought a delicious golden kosher-macrobiotic challah, baked by a Polish woman with a number tattooed on her arm. Abe's Kosher Meats, Moishe's Bakery, and Schacht's Deli were within a half block of my doorstep, God forbid I should be hungry. The Tisch School of the Arts, Cohen's Optical, Felder's Pharmacy, my landlord, Mr. Wertenteil, was Jewish. Even the owners of the Guatemalan crafts shop next door were Jewish. I was home!

I had to find a way to live, to survive. While I studied theatre, I worked as a singing waitress at Sammy's Famous Roumanian Steakhouse. I delivered futons to hundreds of Manhattan walk-ups, schlepped furniture throughout the tri-state area, and drove a car service for Martha Graham, Judy Collins, and Leonard Cohen. I performed in Lower East Side storefronts, and saw as much theatre, art, music, film, poetry readings, and performance art as I could get into. Whether I "second acted" or paid in full, I was becoming a New Yorker, with all the *chutzpah* that entails.

I'd learnt *chutzpah* quickly. My first under-the-table job was as the temporary maitre d' at the Second Avenue Deli. I learnt to use my elbows in half a day. The nice little Kibrew went underground. We're talking survival.

The manager of that first deli job reminded me of my father. He had a wonderful sense of humor, a thick Jewish accent, and a number on his arm that looked eerily familiar. When I called to ask my father whether he knew Issy, he became very excited.

"Issy? Issy Lefkowitz? Does he have red hair? Is he short? Is he funny?"

Yes! It turned out Issy had been in Dad's barracks at Auschwitz. Dad was in faraway New Zealand and had no idea what had become of Issy or any of his other landsmen.

My parents came to visit. Within an hour of our reunion my father was standing outside the Second Avenue Deli window, hands up against the glass, squinting to see inside.

"Is that him, Deborah? Dat chappee dere with the pastrami? No, Deborah you got it wrong. Dat's not Issy. He's not here."

"Dad, that guy's Luis, he's Puerto Rican."

"What about da one with the turkey? Dat's not him, dat chappee is too short. You got it wrong, he's not here."

"That's Mohammad you're pointing at, Dad. He's Bangladeshi."

We lined up outside the restaurant for what seemed like an excruciating amount of time. Once inside, Dad scanned the room. Suddenly he shouted, "Issy," and ran across the restaurant.

Issy didn't remember my father. Dad tried to trigger his memory.

"Remember da chappee with da hunch back? Berish Grinbaum? Yeah? I slept right next to him. What about Srulik Fuchs, the messenger? You remember? He smuggled an apple from one of the Poles and split it four ways with you and Moshe Schertz and me and it was full of worms? Dat was me! Okay, what about when that bastard Zundel beat me to within an inch of my life and *meshuggeneh* Haim Diller was laughing? You remember! And I asked him why he was laughing. And he said, 'It could have been worse, it could have been me!'

But Issy didn't remember. To compensate, he sent over enough food to feed a committee, a big committee.

Now, ten years later, I was making headway in my career. I'd outgrown my job as a singing-telegram *bubbie*. (A singing-telegram *bubbie* demands skills only the most highly trained actors can accomplish. Costume is very important. The thickest pantyhose available, marked with ballpoint pen for varicose veins, eighteen-inch Cabbage-Patch breasts, long and drooping with large red nipples strapped to your chest. Once the *bubbie* housecoat is removed, you perch precariously on the knee of the embarrassed middle-aged man whose birthday it is. At this point I seized poetic license and told dirty jokes to the assembled company. It was excellent on-the-job-training. Training for something, I'm not exactly sure what.)

That was all behind me now. I had already played Sophie Tucker's mother in an off-Broadway musical. The actress who played Sophie was ten years older than I, six inches shorter, and in spite of the fact that she could belt as loud as Sophie Tucker herself, was completely tone-deaf, but who cared? Now I had my Equity card.

I was developing a new solo show. The cast included Charlotte von Rottenberg, a superficial, club-going, German video artist who talks incessantly about art in Euuuuu'wope; Pattie, a midwestern housewife whose obsession with food is only briefly interrupted by a hijacking that occurs on the plane she is on; Dame Diggy McClean, self-proclaimed poet laureate of Australia; Natalie Hennyyoungmanoff, the only Jewish comedienne in Russia; and, finally, a large family of deliciously rich Jewish characters at a bar mitzvah.

I performed at clubs throughout downtown Manhattan. One club had no roof in the backstage area, the dressing room was a tent, the heat provided by fuel-burning lamps.

No matter, each day was wonderful. Each day seemed to present a more resplendent parade of freaks, screwballs, nuts, eccentrics, and geniuses for me to use as material. There was no end to the cavalcade of dingbats, aliens, and village idiots that made up the cornucopia that is New York.

May 1990

Invited to perform my show at the Edinburgh Fringe Festival, and in the midst of preparations, I received an unexpected phone call. It was my parents, offering me (in their words), "The trip of a lifetime! A once-in-a-lifetime opportunity!"

This wasn't a regular vacation. That's not our family. It was a whistle-stop, whirlwind tour of Eastern European death camps. Just my dad and me.

My parents had already undertaken a postwar journey to Poland. Fifteen years earlier, in 1975, the same year I studied drama, the same year of my adult awakening, they had made their way to the forest in Brzozów, Galicia, to visit the site of the massacre of my father's parents.

And now, fifteen years later, my father wanted to return. Here they were, both my parents on the other end of the phone, breathlessly awaiting my reply.

"How's about it, Bebbski? We could go and visit camps, ghettos, prisons. We can go to Brzozów, to the forest. It'll be fun!"

Brzozów. How often had I heard that word? Soccer games, before the war, the family bakery, the river, the school, the Jewish club, the forest.

Would I accompany him to the forest for the unveiling of the long-awaited memorial? It was at the exact same time I was due to go to Edinburgh.

There had never been an official count. No one had known exactly what happened to the eight hundred Brzozów Jews on August 10, 1942.

But in 1975, when my parents nervously made their way through the forest, they were approached by a nun from the nearby orphanage. My mother immediately became highly alarmed. She panicked, certain they were about to be murdered. Instead, the nun delivered the first eyewitness account of the Brzozów genocide since the war.

Eight hundred Jews assembled at the side of the road, marched through the forest, into the woods. That summer morning a young boy from the orphanage silently climbed a tree. He saw the large, freshly dug pit and then watched in silence as German soldiers, aided by Polish collaborators, unleashed a volley of submachine gun bullets into the Jews, into my grandparents and seventy of my relatives.

How could I say no? What about Edinburgh? I couldn't disappoint my father. I suggested we visit the memorial two months later, in October; my father agreed. He wanted to go back again.

Our route was planned. We'd begin in Prague, visit Theresienstadt concentration camp, and then drive through the Czech Republic to Poland, stopping at Auschwitz, Krakow, and finally Brzozów, where Dad's journey began. Then we'd drive back to Prague and fly home.

October 1990

Our hotel and rental car were booked in Prague. We each had a visa for the Czech Republic. On board the Lufthansa overnight flight out of Newark (one survivor I know unwittingly refers to Lufthansa as "Luftwaffe"), my father turned to me and said, "Deborah, I want you to behave yourself while you're here on da trip."

"What do you mean, behave? Dad?"

"I don't want you to cry on da trip. Control yourself."

I agreed to behave myself.

The walls of the Prague airport appeared to have the nicotine residue of all of Eastern Europe. It felt as though we were stepping directly into the past. Aeroflot prop planes, Czech guards smoking on duty, an entire country standing on the quivering new legs of democracy. The tram ticket into the city was one and a half cents. We drove past block after block of ugly apartment buildings, erected alongside noble, crumbling homes, trees, cobblestone streets, the old railway station, graffiti, vandalized statues of Lenin.

When we arrived in the old city, the sun was barely visible above the crisp autumn morning. Our hotel elevator could hold only three. It had a creaky iron gate. After we napped under feather beds in our rooms, we walked through the city and found ourselves in the old Jewish Quarter.

The *Alteneuschule* is the oldest synagogue in Europe. We knocked on the door. A highly nervous old man with no fingers cautiously opened the side door of the synagogue. He spoke only Yiddish. No words were needed. We understood who he was and where he had been.

As I looked through the narrow slits behind the *mechitza*, the thick wall that divides men from women in any Orthodox synagogue, I saw my father reading from the Torah. I felt emotions flow freely from me through the thick stone. The absence was palpable. Once the center of one of the proudest and richest Jewish communities in Europe, now there were barely enough people to complete a service. I sobbed silent tears behind the thickest wall in Prague.

We ate our oversalted duck at dinner the first night in Prague, my father suggesting a tour the next day to the Theresienstadt camp, where he was liberated.

I resisted the idea. I didn't want to share our visit there with anyone. It was private. My father insisted, "We have to let a professional guide show us."

The following day we were on a bus, getting a guided tour of Theresienstadt. The first thing you notice before actually entering the gates of the camp are hundreds of graves. These are graves of survivors who died after their liberation by the Russians. Dad's only surviving brother, Ben, had almost died of typhoid here. Somehow, miraculously, he'd survived. I tried to understand that. Had he died, I would never have known him or my cousins in Sydney.

I could feel my heart beating loudly. How had they survived? I sat in the back of the bus, looking out the window as my father took the microphone and began telling yet another story. Surely the people on the bus understood this manic behavior of his? I skulked in my seat. There were two German tourists on the bus. Why were they there? What did they think? Had they seen my father's number?

At the defunct crematorium in Theresienstadt the old custodian showed us through the building. Someone asked him why he worked there. The old gentleman said he felt it was his privilege to spend his sunset years working in the old crematorium. He was a gentile, a Czech, himself a former inmate of Theresienstadt. Many of his close Jewish friends had died there. It was an act of respect. What overwhelmed him was not the morbid surroundings, it was the never-ending trail of German tourists who, upon seeing the crematoria, asked him why the photographs on exhibit had been fabricated. Germans and other revisionists who repeatedly insisted no one had ever died here. Spoke of their disgust at the deliberate lie they said was being perpetuated.

We returned to Prague in silence. I felt completely exhausted, overwhelmed, deeply grieved. As soon as we stepped off the bus, Dad suggested we visit the Jewish Museum, the Jewish Children's Museum, the Jewish Town Hall, the Jewish cemetery. I wanted some hot soup, to write in my journal, to meditate and reflect on my experience of that morning.

My father argued, why rest? We only had five days in Prague. Time is short!

I was firm. I needed my emotional strength for the camps ahead, for our journey together. He relented, reluctantly.

We tried to get into several restaurants. There seemed to be many empty tables, but no room for us. We hadn't realized the "schemer" method of access, the rubbing of palms to acquire a meal? Finally we actually found a restaurant where we could get hot soup and a grilled cheese sandwich. I was happy we had finally found somewhere to sit. I headed for the ladies' room. There was a long line to use the facilities. Since I'd been living in New York for ten years I knew exactly what to do. I walked into the empty men's room. The porter was furious. No disobeying rules! She berated me loudly and angrily. Disgruntled and dejected, I waited ten minutes to use the ladies' room and finally returned to our table.

"I hate the authority, the abuse, the rules, the acceptance of the status quo. This place is miserable!"

"Deborah, you have to do as you're told here. If you didn't behave yourself in the camps, they'd shoot you!"

I was incredulous. I looked at him, and said, "Dad, we're not in the camps!"

He seemed surprised.

Later, in my hotel room, I wrote an account of the day in my journal. I did not "behave" myself. I could feel years of grief being tapped. I let it flow freely, surprised at the same time by the depths whence it came.

I dried my eyes. They were red and puffy. My father looked at me closely and said nothing. We walked back to the Jewish quarter and toured the Jewish memorials. My father seemed satisfied.

We spent five days together walking, sightseeing, eating salty food when I managed to make a reservation, visiting museums, taking the subway, buying crystal glasses, taking in the spectacular city of Prague. It was the first time we had ever spent any time alone together, and it was a great adventure that we both enjoyed immensely.

Five days later, we drove out of the Czech Republic into Poland. At the border crossing my father chatted with a Polish driver whose car was filled with goods. I was nervous, fantasizing about being stuck at the border in 1939. Where would I have run? We pulled up to the Polish barrier. Our Czech visas were taken away by the officious Polish border guard. We'd overlooked one very important thing. We had needed two Czech visas each, not one, because we were making two separate entries to the Czech Republic. For a moment there seemed no way to return to Prague.

My father panicked.

"Oh dearie me, Deborah. We're in trouble now. What are we gonna do? How are we ever gonna get back? We'll have to leave the car by the side of the road. We'll have to fly from Warsaw. You'll have to forget your birthday in Prague, Deborah. You'll have to cancel that restaurant you booked from New York. You'll have to have your birthday in Gliwice, at the Holiday Inn."

He was panicking, I was trying to reassure him, but the thought occurred to me, "What if he's right? What if I get stuck in Poland for the rest of my life, with Dad?"

After a quick overnight detour to Sosnowiec, the next day we drove to the Czech Consul in Katowice for our visas. Getting new visas was no problem. My father was incredulous. How could it be that easy? How did I find my way? I was annoyed by his negativity, pleased by his compliments. He saw problems around each corner; I had the job of being perky, the problem solver. I understood how difficult my mother's job had been.

We found things easily. People were approachable. I had expected Poland to be cold, gloomy, gray, macabre. Though sunlight only appeared through the smog at noon and disappeared by four o'clock, parts of the Polish countryside were picturesque and beautiful. This was not what I had imagined. People still drove horses and carts. In the cities there was a powerful residue of communism, gray concrete buildings, depressed-looking people, a few empty stores with little merchandise, and bad roads. When we needed directions, drunken taxi drivers and townspeople were not infrequent.

However, the downfall of communism had brought about a fledgling economy. Entrepreneurs were everywhere. We were weary tourists and, in many places, the only tourists.

I'd had a vision of Poland as filled with Jew haters. On our second day I met a kindly woman in a bakery who sold us *ponchkehs*, fresh donuts with plum jam. She herself seemed very sweet. I tried to imagine her betraying Jews and couldn't. The photographer who took our visa photos seemed harmless, too, although we didn't see much of him under the fabric of his very old camera.

That night, a friendly hotel waiter plied us with vodka, the Polish national tonic. I began to relax a little. Perhaps the thing to do was to drink our way through the countryside. That seemed too extreme, but I enjoyed the novelty of getting drunk with my father a couple of times.

The next day, en route to Auschwitz, I asked Dad about the fields we were driving past. Was that corn we could see growing? He looked out of the window, far away. He remembered a young woman attempting escape from the trucks en route on the deportation to Auschwitz from the Krakow ghetto. She had been caught in what looked to him exactly like these fields.

"The guard made her kneel down, put her hands behind her head, and then he shot her in the back of the head. Phew. You're a lucky girl, darling, lucky not to see things like that."

I looked at the fields once more and no longer saw the corn.

As we drove through Poland. Dad was constantly worried we would run out of gasoline even if we had only filled the tank a few hours earlier. No matter how much gas we had, he remained on petrol alert the entire trip. His worst fear was to be stuck in Poland.

Stories rolled out of him, his memories reawakened. Sometimes I wasn't sure if he even knew I was present.

I wanted to share so much with him. I wanted to tell him why I'd cried in my room the day we visited Theresienstadt, how frequently I'd imagined meeting his parents, to speak about my childhood fantasies of murdering Hitler. I wanted to tell him that, somehow, his Holocaust was my Holocaust, too.

Instead I told him other stories of my own survival in New York. My singing waitress job in the rat-infested steak house with the abusive boss, the power-hungry acting teacher, moving furniture to one mafioso's summer home in the Hamptons.

My father knew none of these tales. He was riveted, impressed. Had he known the abusive boss was cussing me out, he said he would have punched the bastard right in the face. I was incredulous. My father was finally championing my vulnerabilities, albeit through past stories.

I had hidden tears from him all my life. Tears proudly held in my chest when I fell off my bike, scraped my knee, got into a fight at school. Invisible behind the walls of the Prague synagogue, kept carefully hidden in the old Krakow ghetto where my father and his brother slept in sewers. And again when he showed me the town square in the same ghetto where one man, a father, selected for life in the ghetto, chose not to be separated from his children and was gunned down with the children on the spot. I saw the entire scene through my father's eyes and contained an ocean of tears. Held at bay in Auschwitz amidst the victims' hair, locked tight in my throat when he showed me his bunk in Birkenau. There, as we walked through the *Arbeit Macht Frei* gate, past the old barbed wire fences, into room after room of old eyeglasses, prostheses, suitcases, photographs, medical laboratories, torture chambers, tragedy, my tears were hidden from view.

While we were in the "museum" of the gas chamber at Auschwitz, a Polish teacher was taking a group of school children through. I wondered what my father was feeling.

We drove over to Birkenau. There we saw his old barracks, his old bunk, or where his bunk had been. An old stove was there now. He was disappointed. "Gee, they didn't keep my bunk. Whaddaya know...."

He showed me where Issy slept.

It began to get dark. "Come on Deborah, let's go! I got locked in here once before, I don't want to get locked in again!"

Two days later, we drove into the Brzozów town square. That morning in the rental car I had finally asked my father for permission to cry at my grandparents' mass grave.

"How long do you think you'll cry?" he had asked.

"Fifteen minutes?"

"Okay, fifteen minutes is okay."

"Thanks, Dad."

We felt the unfriendly eyes of Polish townspeople in the square. What did we want? Hadn't we had enough? A man with a beret recognized my father immediately, and Dad remembered both the man and his brother. This man had been a neighbor, later a slave laborer in Germany. He walked us past Uncle Mendel's soda store in the direction of the old Filler house. Dad's family had buried its fortune in U.S. dollars under the dirt floor in Uncle Mendel's ice storage basement. When they went back to dig it up four years later it had all rotted.

We rounded a corner. A large apartment building loomed, three stories high. I was stunned. My father was from a respected family, the biggest bakery in town, but this was nothing like I'd imagined.

The family bakery was now a butcher shop, closed on this sunny Monday. Dad warned me, "Don't go near, Deborah!"

I ignored him, walking toward the door of the apartment building. I wanted to go in, enter the old family home, find something that belonged to us.

The former neighbor warned me not to go into the building.

He was earnest. Both men insisted I come away from the door. "Don't make trouble, Deborah."

What would I have seen? How would I have known what was ours? I wanted to stand up to "them," show no fear.

But I'm a good girl. I behaved myself.

We ate pierogi in the only restaurant in town. The restaurateur, recently returned from four years in Philadelphia, could say only four words in English.

"Cashier! Philadelphia! Knife! Fork!"

With my father acting as translator, the ex-Philadelphia cashier asked what I did for a living. My father, miming my playing a guitar said, "She's an entertainer."

The cashier offered me a job on the spot. Why not return to Brzozów, be an entertainer in his restaurant? I could move into his house. He was recently divorced and had a lot of extra space. The town had so many opportunities, he told me. Come, bring my U.S. dollars to Brzozów, he said. Move back. I thought, now that's a career move!

Dad went and bought candles and we drove together on the last leg of our journey before turning back to Krakow and

Prague. At the forest, half a mile from town, a small marker sat on the side of the road. Until recently it was the only commemoration of the slaughter.

The Catholic orphanage lay at the foot of the forest. I saw a new path leading up into the trees. As I stepped out of the car and walked toward the path, Dad began to act very strangely. He darted into the orphanage yard, past a pregnant woman hanging washing, behind several beehives, up a hill, into the undergrowth. He seemed to be running in circles, twigs, leaves, and branches snapping underfoot. I called to him, but he didn't answer.

"The path is this way, Dad."

"How do you know? I have to find a nun. She'll show us where it is."

"It's here, I can see it. Dad? Where are you going?"

"The nun will know. Get a nun, Deborah, she'll show us where."

Soon a kindly nun was leading us up the hill to the site, a dachshund at her heels. As I walked behind my father, I wondered if he needed a nun from the orphanage to escort him to his parents' grave.

The memorial lay in a clearing in the forest, blanketed in thousands of dead leaves. It looked like many forests I had seen, like the Berkshires, only with bones. The memorial was a rough concrete square with a blue wrought iron Star of David and marble plaque. A few chrysanthemums stood in bottles on a ledge behind the plaque. The nuns regularly tended the grave and left flowers from their garden. I gave the nun all the Polish money I had in an impotent gesture of thanks. She thanked us and quietly left.

We stood in an eerie silence and then set about trying to stand the candles upright so that they could be lit. Each time we attempted to stand them up, they fell over, again and again. Is it only Polish candles that will not stand up? It seemed like a bad Polish joke, absurd and monstrously funny at the same time.

After more than twenty minutes we managed finally to erect and light six lone candles.

I suggested we say *Kaddish*, the prayer for the dead.

"My yalmulke! My prayer book! I forgot my *tallis* in the car, Deborah!"

I suggested we recite the *Kaddish* without a prayer book.

My father agreed and began to recite the prayer. For a second his voice caught in his throat. Right then, at that very moment, I began quietly to weep. Tears came flowing out as they had never done before. Weeping for innocence and loss, for justice and pain, for my grandparents, Gedaleyeh and Runia, and my uncles, Tuciu and Selig and Ben and Leib and Mendel. For us all.

It was the first time I ever truly wept in the presence of my father. It felt like an enormous relief. As I wept, my father kicked away the autumn leaves, looking to see if there were any bones still visible. I wept and he kicked. Weeping and kicking, kicking and weeping.

Through my tears I chanted for strength, for forgiveness, for wisdom. After several minutes, something stirred in me. What was it? I listened.

I heard something say to me, "It's enough. Let go. Be free. Enough of mourning. Enjoy your life!"

Could it be? I felt as though this was the pivotal moment of my whole life. I listened again and squinted into the forest. Where were they? I could feel them near. I felt an incredible strength come over me and, in that moment, made a determination to do my utmost to make sure that the world would never forget what had happened to them. Do something, somehow not to let the world simply forget Runia and Gedaleyeh Filler, their family, their neighbors, and their peers. Somehow they would not die nameless, in impotence, in vain.

We quietly stood. Before we left the grave, I asked my father if there was anything he would like to say here.

Without hesitation he said yes. I can't recall his exact words, but I remember how moved I felt by how he addressed them that day amidst the leaves in the forest.

"Mum, Dad...I've missed you all dese years. I'm sorry what happened to you, how you died. I'm sorry I couldn't help you somehow. I missed you all dese years. I wish you could have been in New Zealand. You would have had a good life dere. I am happy dere. I would be able to visit your grave dere. I wanted to come back and make sure tings were all right. Now you have a gravestone. I don't tink I'll be coming back, though you never know...so, anyway, dat's it. Goodbye. Rest in peace. I love you."

We returned to New York ,and a few days later my father departed for New Zealand. I started to think immediately about honoring my commitment. I perform comedy. How could I use humor to honor them? The Holocaust had no humor.

November 1990

I began work on a show. At first, performing embarrassingly bad Polish jokes in a Lower East Side shopfront/theatre, friends advised me to dig more deeply, to find my own voice, not to be afraid.

I told a publicist I knew that I was working on a humorous piece about the Holocaust. He warned me that if it weren't brilliant, I'd have to leave town. No pressure.

I began to improvise my darkest fantasies, a slave laborer, an inmate of Auschwitz, a starving child. Was I crazy? It would have been so much easier to parody Tammy Faye Bakker.

With the greatest of trepidation, I continued. During one rehearsal, a child ghost appeared just as I was improvising entering the gates of Auschwitz. "Deb! I'm so hungry. Did you bring something to eat? We've been waiting for you to come back, all of us. Do you have cheesecake?"

This macabre character later became my imaginary child, Chaikeh, in my off-Broadway show, *Punch Me in the Stomach!*

May 1991

I was a bundle of nerves before my first workshop at La Mama Theatre. A Buddhist told me to go onstage with the energy of Mahalia Jackson across my chest. It worked.

November 1991

We had rewritten the piece. Playwright Israel Horvitz called it, "Extraordinary," in the *Village Voice*. New York Theatre Workshop offered to produce it. I had an impending tour of Australia and New Zealand.

February 1992

My director and co-writer, Alison Summers, recommended giving my parents a copy of the piece to read before they saw it, with a reminder that plays are not literal. Both parents read the entire play and returned it to me in a half-hour.

My father's sole comment was that I definitely should not use my first boyfriend Kevin's real name. After all, he said, Kevin could sue me. My mother agreed with my father. They were appeased when I offered to add an "l" and change Kevin's name to Kelvin.

March 1992

After the opening in Wellington, my father came onto the stage with flowers. We embraced. There was not a dry eye in the house.

The next night on national television news, the news reader announced, "New Zealand girl pokes fun at the Jewish Holocaust, coming up after the break." My parents were mortified. They attacked me, telling me that the whole Jewish community of New Zealand was up in arms, all six of them! My parents and I had an important discussion about the ratio of positive to negative coverage to expect from the media. I guessed 80 percent would be positive and 20 percent would not. Agreeing, my parents and sister backed me for the run and the world tour that continued off and on for several years. I'll always be grateful for their support.

April 1992

Closing night after the show in Auckland. We had done several interviews together. My father handled the press like a professional. He was in his element. Celebrities, politicians, the mayor, old neighbors, ex-school friends, our family doctor, members of my parents' bowling club, Rotary, lodges, and the general public attended the sold-out shows in droves. Many flocked to shake my father's hand, which was not difficult since my parents came to every show. Champagne was sent to our table several nights after the show by appreciative audience members. In the show my father was a survivor celebrity, and now life was imitating art. He'd been my hero; now he was everybody's hero.

As my father helped us dismantle the set, he suddenly looked at me. He told me thank you. "I'm very proud of you." That was a moment I shall never forget.

November 2000

My father died last September. As his hands skittered across the hospital blanket, I knew he was replaying his life. Each morning he awoke more exhausted. He told us he was baking challah in his dreams.

Words cannot express the extent of my loss. It is too great. Up until his last moment he gave the gift of love. His dying words were a blessing on my sister and on me. The last thing he said to me was, "I bless you with all my heart and with all my soul."

My last words to my father as he traveled across to the far shore, were in Yiddish. "*Gei Schaja, gei in a Zeisse Schluf.* Go into a sweet sleep. *Wir Leiben dich.* We love you. *Wir kimmen.* We're coming. We love you. *A vielen dank Tateh.* Thank you, Dad." He went home, absent no more.

DEB FILLER is a Toronto-based New Zealander. She was a founding member of New Zealand's fringe theater group, "Debbie and the Dum Dums." She studied theater in New York and made her off-Broadway debut in the musical-comedy, *Sophie*. Her sold-out one-woman show, *Filler-Up*, is performed throughout North America. She also performed *Punch Me in the Stomach!* and won Critics' Pick at the New Zealand International Festival of the Arts.

To Mothers.
To my mother, Sherena Kallus Frenkel
To my sister, Hedy Samet, and her children,
Yitzchak and Goldy, who share in this legacy
To my daughters, Candice and Lisa
And finally,
To my husband, Robert, with whom I share everything.

Chapter 6

TRACES ALONG A BROKEN LINE

Vera Loeffler

Through her photographs, Vera Loeffler captures loss, love, and longing. Her ability to hold on to memory is original and beautifully expressed in her work. We have been friends for over thirty years, and her desire for excellence and perfection are still her mainstay in everything she touches. —MW

I was born on September 12, 1942, in Bekescaba, Hungary. For as far back as memory takes me, my nuclear family was composed of three females—my mother, my sister, and myself.

Acquaintance with my father was made solely through photographs, supplemented by the oral history of those who survived the Holocaust.

My mother was an enterprising woman. She managed to escape from Communist Hungary—virtually alone with two children—to establish a life in "America."

My mother—beautiful, ever dignified, ever sorrowful.

The loss of love and loved ones left an infinite vacuum filled with this sorrow. As children, my sister and I wrestled with the need to protect her and the intolerance we felt for her limitless pain, predictably at hand on the periphery of every happy moment.

We had not yet realized that her melancholy could be absorbed—if somewhat altered—by us. We eventually integrated her suffering, and it changed us.

My mother died in November of 1999, just missing the new century.

I knew her only as "Mother."

There was much integral that she left submerged. The woman never surfaced.

In searching for that woman I have turned to old photographs, becoming a time traveler to places her thoughts had revisited at the end of her life—to a past she quietly invited me to see with her.

In the end I am left with a tapestry of disjointed images that map her history. The rest is a fiction to illuminate more than it distorts.

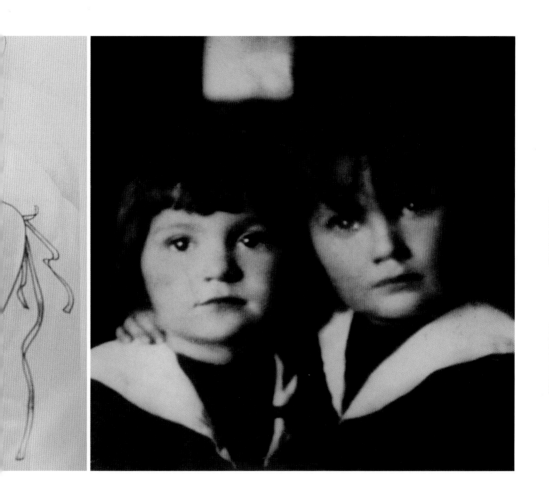

Your speech assumes the waveless dynamic of the dead

Rolling through a space

Raging and racing frontal footprints

Pancho and Maria in perpetuity

On the last leg of some neuronal midnight run.

I read "Genetic Mapping Complete"

To recall where you still live

Eyes hazel, hair blonde, unopinionated.

But I inconsolably crave the carnal

Of breath-heat and surprise

And the comfort, on waking,

Of tripping on a boundless love based in nothing

That I am

Save for those mappings.

Candice Loeffler

Born in Bekescaba, Hungary, **VERA LOEFFLER** studied photography at the Corcoran School of Art in Washington, D.C. She has exhibited her photography in the individual exhibit, "Old Baby Series," and several group exhibits, including the Photography Invitational and "Romantic Image: Two Cities." She has won first place in the black and white category in the *Washington Post* Annual Photography Contest. She is currently a freelance photographer and works as a curator of private collections.

Aviva Kempner and Helen Ciesla Covensky, mother

Grandmother Helen Ciesla

Dedicated to
my grandparents and aunt we never knew,
Helen, Leon, and Cesia Ciesla
and Hannah Pokempner,
and to the inspiring survival and accomplishments
of my uncle, David Ciesla Chase,
and my beloved mother, Helen Ciesla Covensky,
and her beautiful paintings.

Chapter 7

KEEPING THE FAMILY NAME ALIVE

Aviva Kempner

Filmmaker Aviva Kempner explores her personal history in her groundbreaking film, Partisans of Vilna. *Her generosity to everyone, but particularly to artists, from all over the world, is legendary. Her new award-winning film,* The Life and Times of Hank Greenberg, *is a must see. —MW*

Amid the rubble of the Third Reich, a Lithuanian-born American soldier, shocked by the annihilation of Eastern European Jewry and his mother's death, was compelled to write feature stories about holidays miraculously being celebrated by the survivors in Berlin—their first free Passover seder in thirteen years, and their first Jewish New Year services since liberation—and the tearfully few family reunions among the displaced Jews. The military journalist's favorite story was about Polish-born Dudek Ciesla, an orphaned survivor of Auschwitz, and his reunion with his blond, green-eyed sister Hanka, who had survived the war by passing as a Polish-Catholic in a forced labor camp near Stuttgart, Germany. Having lost their parents and only other sister at Auschwitz, their reunion took on poignant meaning.

The Jewish G.I. fell in love with the sister. For their wedding ceremony, Hanka Ciesla honored the American liberators who transported her by tank to Berlin by wearing a wedding dress fashioned from a nylon U.S. army parachute. The young bride took her deceased mother's name, Helen, as her own. Ten months later I was born. My picture adorned the front page of an Army newspaper with the dubious title of "Miss 1947," identifying me as the first American Jewish war baby born in Berlin.

My mother decided to give me a Hebrew name in honor of my grandmother, who loved singing Zionist songs in the ancient language. My father's own lore about my naming was that he wanted a *bris*, a ritual circumcision for Jewish males, in Berlin. But since I was a girl, he opted for putting a Hebrew name on his daughter's German birth certificate as an ultimate act of cultural revenge. When I was three and a half years old, we left Germany to settle in the American midwest. My mother vowed never to return to Germany. My mind blocked out any conscious memories of speaking German words and the face of my beloved nanny, Fraulein Shubert.

My brother was born in 1951. As we grew up in Detroit, my mother hardly spoke about the war years to us, because, as she declared: "I wanted to protect you from those terrible times." A mother understandably wants to hide war traumas and horrors from her children.

The climate in America, even in the Jewish community, was not especially receptive to hearing the survivors' harrowing tales. Once the war was over, the message was that life was supposed to go back to normal. Even the European survivors adopted that philosophy. They were preoccupied with making a living and bringing up their families in their adopted land. My mother claims she did not even exchange wartime stories with her sibling. Only in their anguish over President Ronald Reagan's trip to Bitburg, Germany, did my mother tell me that she and my uncle began to reveal their wartime stories to each other.

But a child has a sixth sense about family losses, especially when there are no grandparents or family from earlier generations around the house. Every Jewish holiday I distinctly recollect my mother's pain as she mourned for her parents and sister and their holidays together. I was not taught much about the Holocaust at school. During my thirteenth summer, I first discovered the horror of Auschwitz by reading Leon

Uris's novel, *Exodus,* on a beach in upper Michigan. In one high school English class, we were assigned to read John Hersey's riveting novel about the Warsaw Ghetto uprising, *The Wall.* Although I was the first student to correctly identify the climax of the book—"The Jews in the ghetto realized they would be facing death at Treblinka"—I did not personally associate the gassing of Polish Jews with my own family's demise.

When I started connecting World War II history with my not having grandparents, I wondered why the Americans had not rescued them. One of the few stories my mother did relate is how she believed her father, who had saved her life by obtaining false documents for her, was coming to rescue her at the end of the war. When she saw the American planes flying over the German forced labor camp, my mother figured her heroic father had joined the allied forces.

Since we did not want Mother to relive the war years, it was an unspoken rule to shield her from movies and television shows about World War II. Instead of war movies, Mother made sure that we watched love stories. She had grown up on these classics and conveyed the joy of watching the romantic scenes to her daughter. I remember sitting by her many Sunday afternoons looking at first kisses and confessions of amour. I believe that watching those tales of love always helped mother escape the harsh reality of family losses and reminded her of happy prewar moments when she went to the movies with her girlfriends.

My mother reminisced about how much she enjoyed watching Shirley Temple films in her youth. She herself was called "Shirley Temple" by an American friend in Detroit because of her curly locks. Years later, she delighted in meeting my brother's next-door neighbor over the terrace divide because he was none other than Shirley Temple's son. Mother beamed while telling him, "I grew up in Poland watching your mother on the screen." I could not help thinking that images of that child star also helped my mother through the terrible war years.

As a teenager, I fantasized about fighting and killing Nazis. Kill one for the dead grandparents we never knew. Kill another for our parents' nightmarish memories and lifelong anxieties.

I was fascinated with angst films about "the war," searching the screen for positive Jewish characters I could identify with in my own life. Millie Perkins in *The Diary of Anne Frank* (1959) and Rod Steiger in *The Pawnbroker* (1965) were obvious favorites. While watching the 1966 Academy Awards ceremony in my college dorm, I sobbed tears of disappointment when Lee Marvin's hilarious portrayal of a drunken cowboy in *Cat Ballou* beat Rod Steiger's riveting performance as a haunted Holocaust survivor in *The Pawnbroker* for best actor. I felt personally betrayed.

Watching *Roots* in 1977 and *Holocaust* in 1978, I became intrigued about my own roots. During a 1979 Thanksgiving visit to Detroit, I leafed through Lujan Dobroszycki and Barbara Kirshenblatt-Gimblett's *Image before My Eyes*, a photo essay book about Polish-Jewish life between the wars. A burning desire to explore my family's past was kindled. After rereading Leon Uris's *Mila 18*, a book on the Warsaw Ghetto uprising, I felt struck to make a film about Jewish resistance against the Nazis, a topic that became the focus of my life's work.

I dropped my legal-lobbying career advocating Native American treaty rights to make a movie about unknown stories of Jewish partisans. I formed a nonprofit foundation, giving it my grandparents' name, Ciesla, to keep the memory of the family name alive. The uncle who had survived the war as Dudek Ciesla, and had become one very successful David Chase in America, provided the seed money for my "roots" film.

My mother, who had successfully shielded us from her war stories, was horrified by my desire to explore the forbidden topic. Objecting vehemently to my career change, she claimed her hold over the painful memories. She was claiming her perfect right to control her memories as well as my knowledge of them. But I was determined that opening the Pandora's box of those memories was exactly the path I needed to follow to grasp her pain. And, possibly, to lessen the inherited guilt of being the child of a survivor.

My abrupt and passionate decision to make a movie about Jewish resistance was not so unusual. A pattern had emerged all over the world: artistically minded children of Holocaust survivors chose to document the Holocaust on film before the survivors died. Some, like me, never heard detailed tales about the war, while others grew up with such tales as their bedtime stories. An international group of Jewish filmmakers was motivated to document their parents' past or an aspect of the Holocaust that ordinarily would have been ignored.

More often than not, we had only Hollywood's images of the war with the many stories of suicidal and dysfunctional survivors. Writers, who themselves had not experienced the Holocaust firsthand, seem to believe such horrid experiences could *only* produce absolute madness or the desire to commit suicide, especially in women. This ubiquitous portrayal perpetuates the literary and cinematic image of the Jew as helpless victim. While the leading female Holocaust survivors in both *Sophie's Choice* (1982) and *Enemies, a Love Story* (1989) kill themselves rather than endure living with painful memories, in *The Pawnbroker*, Rod Steiger, haunted by his memories and barely functioning in the real world, remains among the living. Israeli films also reinforce this stereotype by depicting female

Holocaust survivors as hopelessly *meshuggeneh*. In a Jewish nation, the only haven for Jews during and after the war, such a persona belittles the significant contribution survivors have made to Israel.

Fictitious melodramas may be sensational, and perhaps commercially successful, but the more mundane stories of the Holocaust survivors who picked up the pieces of their lives after the war are the true dramas. Surely, survivors had emotional difficulty coping with their horrific experiences. There is no way to be exposed to such massive trauma without scars. But what is incredible is that thousands upon thousands of Holocaust survivors started new lives by immediately finding mates and starting families in faraway lands like America, Australia, and Israel, or among the ruins of war-torn Europe, especially Germany.

In fact, my role model for changing careers was my own mother, who began painting colorful and life-affirming abstract expressionist works after her children went to college. She claimed, "each stroke was for one of the six million," in paintings containing beautiful images. My uncle, an Auschwitz survivor who became a very successful businessman and philanthropist, was another inspiring example for me.

I also had other positive role models growing up among my parents' European friends. Many of them were survivors who had made lives for themselves as professors, psychiatrists, businessmen, and doctors. What I saw in my own mother, my relatives, and my mother's survivor friends were vibrant women and men with sad pasts, but a strong drive to raise their children and persevere in spite of their experiences.

For me they were and always will remain an inspiration.

I believe that film is the most vivid conveyor of culture and imagery in our society. In today's world we often learn more from the visual imagery of movies and television than from the written word. That is why I am so concerned about how the Holocaust in general, and the survivors in particular, are portrayed on screen.

This concern motivated me to make a movie about the unexplored topic of Jewish resistance against the Nazis. Impressed with Josh Waletzky's talent in directing the film version of *Image before My Eyes* (1980), I asked him to direct this documentary on Jewish resistance. My original intention was to explore the unfair question, "Why didn't Jews fight back?" Waletzky and I discovered that the real question was, "How did they resist while facing such crushing odds?" The premiere of *Partisans of Vilna* (1986) at the Berlin Film Festival was poetic justice—seeing the Ciesla name on the screen in the belly of the beast.

My Ph.D.-like pursuit of knowledge about the Holocaust made me more aware of the liberties taken in popular literature and films about it. Leon Uris's books and the mini-series, *Holocaust*, contributed greatly to general American awareness of World War II horrors. And although these works personally inspired exploration of my own "roots," I am wary of most fictionalized depictions of the period because they usually contain gross inaccuracies that are mistaken for fact. Researching *Partisans of Vilna,* I quickly realized that the literary license Uris took in plotting *Mila 18*—like the "gentile" Polish woman so valiantly aiding her lover, the Jewish resistance leader—was contrary to the reality: too few non-Jews assisted the Jewish freedom fighters in Warsaw, Vilna, or anywhere else in Europe.

Many viewers of *Partisans of Vilna* were moved by the aging witnesses; the partisans' demeanor reminded audience members of their own Yiddish-speaking grandparents. Ironically, poet Abba Kovner, the leader of the Jewish resistance in the Vilna ghetto and the chief witness in *Partisans of Vilna*, refused at first to be filmed because he thought people would not believe such old-looking survivors had been resistance fighters. But after seeing the oral testimonies interspersed in the movie, *Reds*, Kovner agreed that only eyewitnesses, even forty years after the war, could tell the stories.

The public was impressed that "everyday, regular folk," so unlike the *Rambo* and Schwarzenegger types of Hollywood movies, committed heroic acts. In fact, women's truths can be stronger than such macho fiction. There are depictions of strong-willed and courageous political women in *Partisans of Vilna*. During World War II, a courageous female courier, Vitka Kempner (no relation to author), led the first act of armed Jewish resistance in Eastern Europe. With two male comrades, she smuggled homemade bombs out of the Vilna ghetto and planted them on railroad tracks. When a German train was blown up, her Jewish resistance organization, worried about Nazi retaliation in the Vilna ghetto, could not acknowledge the feat. A Polish group had the *chutzpa* to claim responsibility and the accompanying glory. Risking their lives as couriers and partisans during the war, these female underground fighters went on to become a psychologist, an Israeli Parliament member, a shopkeeper, and a school teacher.

The present-day emphasis on Holocaust education in schools, and the success of the U.S. Holocaust Memorial Museum, has created a climate more sensitive to less sensational and more realistic portraits of Holocaust survivors. In America we are finally able to embrace the lessons of the Holocaust and not shy away from the pain of the survivors or feel guilty about being spared their horrible experiences.

Making movies on Holocaust subjects is not the exclusive province of the second generation born of the ashes, but it fulfills a psychological need in us to commemorate the dead. Maybe if I had heard war stories growing up I never would have chosen to examine what happened during the Holocaust. To make up for the loss of our families, we create celluloid substitutes that help fill in the gaps.

As I was finishing this essay a familiar call came—my mother telephoning me to watch an old-time romance, this one starring Kirk Douglas, Kim Hunter, and Walter Matthau, on television. As the credits rolled, we compared notes about the movie's sad ending. She recalled how we had often watched great Hollywood love stories together while I was growing up, and how those will always be her favorites. Kisses on the silver screen still remain the "great escape" from wartime memories. No wonder I make movies to comprehend the pain of my mother's past.

I, the granddaughter of Helen Ciesla, needed to unlock the dark past. And in our family, my brother, Jonathan, was given the middle name, Leon, for our murdered grandfather, just as I was given the middle name, Helen, after our maternal grandmother. And when he became a father, Jonathan gave his middle daughter, Delaney, the middle name, Ciesla, to honor our grandparents who perished without our ever having known them.

AVIVA KEMPNER, a writer and filmmaker, produced and co-wrote *Partisans of Vilna*. She produced, wrote, and directed *The Life and Times of Hank Greenberg* which was awarded top honors by the National Society of Film Critics, the National Board of Review, the New York Film Critics Circle, and Broadcast Film Critics Association.

Ms. Kempner is a recipient of the 1996 Guggenheim Fellowship for filmmaking. She writes film criticism and feature articles for numerous publications, including *The Boston Globe*, *The Forward*, *Washington Jewish Week,* and the *Washington Post*.

Standing: Leo Laufer, brother; Janina Laufer, mother; Sylvia Laufer Goldberg;
Peter Goldberg, husband. Seated: Yoni, Uri, and Eli.

Joseph Laufer, father

Dedicated to
the beloved memory of my father, Joseph Laufer,
and in honor of my dear mother, Janina Laufer

Chapter 8

FAMILY MYTHOLOGY

Sylvia Goldberg

Sylvia Goldberg, my dear childhood friend, says so much in what she cannot allow herself to say. Her strength and courage shine through every unspoken word. —MW

"Speech after long silence; it is right."

W. B. Yeats

I had no idea why, one day last spring, I found myself visiting the Goethe Institute. I did not remember ever seeing it there, before I passed it, walking down Seventh Street in Washington, D.C., where I live. I knew, of course, what it was, having seen ads many years ago in the *Times* announcing

German cultural events taking place at the larger New York branch. On this particular day I passed it by once before retracing my steps. There was certainly a force that drew me again to its entrance. I did not allow myself time to reject the pull. Once inside I was chilled. I felt anxious. It seemed to me that I was actually visiting Germany. What did I come for? What was I planning to find? All around me in the lobby were paintings, but it felt wrong to stop and admire them. Anywhere else I would likely have been drawn to contemplate the colors and forms. Yet, I was not in search of German culture. Not enough time it seemed could ever pass for that sort of quest.

I would have exited then had it not been for that offer of assistance from a young woman at the information desk. She was no native Washingtonian, gauging by the unmistakable Teutonic clip to her speech. So now I cast about for a response, not wishing to appear rude by departing wordlessly. What did I really need? Nothing I knew about before the instant she asked. And then suddenly it crystallized—I could use a city map of Munich, startling myself even as I was forming the words. Secretly, I was pleased at my quick thinking. This polite request apparently was one she was eager to fulfill. She even volunteered to help me acquire all manner of useful information, for assuredly, she had me pegged as a future tourist to that capital of Bavaria. That she could not have come to a less likely conclusion struck me as wholly ironic.

Munich was a place I had left, not one to which I was headed. Even though I asked for the map, I felt awkward being in possession of it. I shared with no one in my family any part of that encounter. As always, when flitting around the periphery of the Holocaust, I felt the need to keep it private. I did not drop the map in the nearest receptacle either, probably because of a mystical bent of mine that has me analyzing and reviewing events to determine whether they possess inherently broader significance than the ostensibly simple one we first glimpse. I set a goal then—I would use the map to locate the street where I grew up.

I knew the name of the street. I may even have known it as a very young child when we all lived there. My Polish mother and father, my brother and me, who were born there, lived in an apartment in town. But trying to locate the street without knowing its spelling became a near hopeless venture. The unfolded glossy map was huge; it had historical references to the city's medieval origins and contained beautiful illustrations of its outstanding features. As to its significance in the damning chapter of modern history, not a word. Its very innocuousness seemed to mock. One should not expect more of a tourist promo, I reckoned. I did, however, seize on the proud description of the rapid transit trains marked by the letter "S." If one wished, one could ride the "S" train to the airport or to Dachau, just to visit, of course.

Leaving my first home, almost at the age of five, gave me the advantage of actually remembering the names of parks where childhood memories hazily resurrected an idyllic scene of gazing at swans, of gathering flowers that magically transformed themselves into a crown of daisies for my head. I looked carefully at the streets in the grids near Hirschgarten Park and Nymphenburg Palace, but I could not be sure. It became important to me, I had to find a spot on a map. For me it would be like retrieving a missing snapshot in a family album.

It occurred to me that if I could just see it spelled correctly somewhere I would certainly find it. But where to begin? This was not the first time since my father's death that I wished I could ask him just one more thing. But I always felt his strong presence in my life, and I knew if I delved into his past the answer would be clear. And it was. My father was the most organized person I have ever known, and after I thought about his files and stamps, I knew where to look.

My late father's enormous yellowing prayer book made the ocean voyage with us to America. It was part of his legacy that made its way into my home. As I held it in my hands I felt his essence, even in the way he preserved the fragile binding. On the inside cover, just as I had envisioned, were the bright blue stamped words: *Josef, Laufer, Munchen, Isensteinstrasse.* With that bit of detective work out of the way, I got out the map, located the landmarks, and uncovered the street exactly in the vicinity of those verdant parks.

How did I feel? Incomplete. So, I had found the street, studied the town. It was enough of a trip back. What memories does a child hold? It was more the told history than the remembered account that filled my mind. How could I have known then that my parents, upon their liberation by the Russians, opted instead to seek the safe haven of the American sector of Germany. It was, of course, not the ultimate destiny in their trajectory from Poland to Germany. In due time that interlude was succeeded by the globe-stretching migration to the west coast of the United States. It was a breathtaking transformation. A positive, life-affirming resettlement. Yet, we came with our history intact.

There was no reticence when it came to imparting the stories of the almost unendurable suffering during the war. They were told to us so that we should have that all-important knowledge. We also did not have to wonder at our dearth of relatives, their faces were recalled in the rare photographs that survived in the possession of a more "fortunate" relative who had endured the war in the relative safety of England.

In the 1950s, Los Angeles saw the arrival of many similar refugee families, and as was their tendency, they banded together according to country of origin. It was not just we who heard other languages spoken at home, who knew nothing of American cuisine, it was our new friends as well. As an adjunct to some of these other facts of our lives, almost down to the last refugee family, the number of children they had was two. Some of my "American" friends had larger families. It was something we accepted.

We were close to our parents, and we were cherished by them, for they were the only family we had. We were happy in our existence, lucky to be free of deprivation. The trouble was, by the time we reached our preteen years, we thought we had absorbed a great many things about our parents' desperate times: my father's punishing years as a slave laborer, my mother's constant flight to conceal her true identity. But there were entire chapters as yet unaddressed. It did not occur to us that there was still the possibility of new anguish.

I still do not recall the sequence of events that led up to the discussion I had with my mother, but during that exchange she revealed to me that not only was she my beloved father's second wife, but that he also had been a father to some other little girls. I could not bear the thought. To my childish mind it seemed like a betrayal. Did he not refer to me as *die goldene*, his golden child? There were photographs. Two serious, beribboned, dark-haired girls with their heads inclined toward each other. Did I really resemble the older one? My jealousy was short-lived, however. In an amazingly brief time I came to view this new revelation as something positive. It would set me apart from my peers, it would lend me a certain cachet. Realizing that my mother was not adversely affected by the knowledge that she was not the first, I took a similar stance and then took it further. I made them my sisters. Suddenly, I came from a larger family. I managed to share this "secret" with many of my friends and turned this initial heartache into something else entirely. In fact, I had always longed for an older sister, so now I had two. This special fantasy had to substitute for the real thing. Unless, of course, the corollary fantasy came true—that through some miracle they had survived and would soon appear.

This memory of that time overtook me when I was looking up the street spelling in the old *siddur*. Although I knew where to look for that, because undoubtedly I had seen it many years earlier, there was something else for which I was absolutely unprepared. There, on the flyleaf, in my father's bold and achingly familiar hand in Hebrew, appeared the names, *Rivka and Mindl,* and accompanying them, the following: *daughters of Yosef Meir, Yahrzeit, 26th of Elul.*

I absorbed the terrible sadness of that inscription. It was quite a shock to read it, for surely he had never spoken of them to me, ever. I reflected on when he might have decided to record their names and surely with a heavy heart. Did he record it for himself? Did he think maybe someday I would come across their names? These are not among the questions I wished I could have asked him.

I thought again about the map. How I mused over the serendipitous way in which it came into my possession. So this was the justification, or perhaps only the reason I requested it on that visit to the Institute. It was a catalyst. Much more than pinpointing a location, that map was the vehicle I rode to reach my father's spirit again. It was his weathered *siddur* and his elegant script that evoked within me the image of his warmth and the knowledge of his wisdom.

While he shared his life with me, it was only within the circle of our family that he entrusted his recollections. He was a most private man, full of dignity. As I reveal the only glimpse I had of the foreshortened lives of two young girls, I would ask his acceptance of my need to share this knowledge. My longing for him, for the two little sisters I will never know, stays with me.

Born in Munich, Germany, and raised in Los Angeles, **SYLVIA GOLDBERG** works in tourism as a professional bilingual Hebrew guide in Washington, D.C. She has also been a writer and editor at *Near East Report* in Washington, D.C., and a freelance writer for the *Baltimore Jewish Times*.

*I would like to dedicate this work to the past, present,
and future of the Jaskovits-Chanes family*

*The past is the roots
The present is the trunk
The future is the fruit*

*The Future
Adir Joseph Weisel, Raphael Moshe Weisel, Gavriel
Shlomo Weisel, Chanan Weisel, Yididya Weisel, Tzur Weisel*

*The Present
Eugene Jason-Jaskovits, Jutta Chanes Jason-Jaskovits*

*The Past
Joszef Jaskovits, 55; Hinda Rifka Jaskovits, 53;
Majsi Jaskovits, 35; Babcsi Jaskovits, 35; Ilanka Jaskovits, 30;
Moshe Jaskovits, 9; Esther Jaskovits, 7
Abe Gottliebb, 31; Sari Gottliebb, 29
Abe and Sari had six children
Sari was pregnant with her seventh child
All died in Auschwitz in May 1944*

*Joseph Chanes, 80, Died in September 1945
From a gunshot wound sustained in May 1945
Gita Chanes, 55, Died in 1954*

Chapter 9

STARTING OVER

Rosie Weisel

Rosie Weisel, my lovely sister-in-law, lives on a kibbutz in Israel. Rosie is an only child who now has six sons of her own. Her intimate diary of coming to terms with her personal history is profound and most touching. —MW

I am afraid I don't know quite where to start. I have many mixed emotions. Right now, I feel sad. I watched a movie yesterday called *The Music Box*, a Holocaust movie. My fifteen-year old son, Gavi, brought it home from the library. We watched it together. Very powerful. Too powerful. Too much pain.

Not a good idea to have watched the movie. It brings me into a world that I usually like to put away. Deep down where no one can see the pain I carry around from that world, that has come to be known as the Holocaust. Each time I enter that world, it literally sucks out the living energy that I need to function in everyday life. It leaves me sad and heavy. Heavy with all the hurt and pain of so many people killed. So many families destroyed. A great, great tragedy.

I usually say, enough! You have no time to sit here now with these feelings, Rose. You have so much to do. You need to leave this Holocaust world behind. Start thinking positive thoughts. Reenergize yourself with the beauty that exists all around you. Focus on being positive and raising my six boys. I mentally fold up my Holocaust world and place it back into the deep crevices of my mind until the next time. And there will be a next time. There always seems to be a next time. Even looking at the beautiful face of my youngest son, Tzur. So round and full of life—such a happy little boy. Then those thoughts seep in. How many round, beautiful faces were destroyed? How many mothers looking lovingly into their children's eyes were destroyed? Mothers searching for the right words to explain away the horrors wrought by a generation of evil.

Day 2

I feel much better this morning. The heavy sadness I felt yesterday after watching the movie has receded into the background. It's 3:12 A.M. and the house is quiet. A house safely cradling my sons. Two of my sons have moved into their adult worlds outside the warmth of this house and are doing fine.

This is my time. My personal time, when I can choose to do almost anything. Sometimes I read. Sometimes I pray. Sometimes I exercise. Sometimes I fold laundry. Almost every morning I check e-mail and do my La Leche League work.

Sometimes I choose to put on my earphones and enter a very private special world of music. I play the piano loudly. It's just me and the music. I am forty-seven years old and learning to play the piano. We bought the piano for our twenty-fifth wedding anniversary and my forty-fifth birthday. I make space for it in my small home on the kibbutz where I live, in Israel.

I always wanted to play piano. But when I was a young girl, we didn't have money for the luxury of piano lessons, much less a piano. I was okay with that fact. It was part of the givens of my childhood. I didn't seem to mind it much.

When I was about eight, I would go with my good friend, Janet Waterstone, to her piano lessons once a week, on the way home from school. I would wait outside the door for a half an hour listening to the beautiful music, after which we would walk a couple of blocks to her grandmother's house for cookies and milk, just like in the movies. Going to Janet's grandmother's after school was a daily ritual.

Janet's grandmother lived in a large colonial house with lots of rooms. And, of course, there was a piano on which Janet could practice. I spent many wonderful times with Janet at her grandmother's. Janet and I were very good friends and I decided to adopt her grandmother. She is the first grandmother I remember adopting. I would subsequently adopt a few more grandparents, parents, and sometimes whole families along the way. But Janet's grandmother was the first. She seemed perfect. Of course, this was from the perspective of an eight-year-old only child without grandparents of her own. I have painted this picture-perfect memory of Janet's grandmother with gray hair, cookies and milk, a big colonial house, and a piano. And what a warm memory it is.

Day 3—two weeks later, July 12, 2000

It's very interesting how the writing of this chapter is taking shape, with day-by-day recordings. Recordings of my thoughts and feelings, and first recollected thoughts about hearing about the Shoah—the Holocaust.

I was in sixth grade, twelve years old. I was an independent child, what people would probably refer to today as a "latchkey kid." I was an only child with two very hard-working parents. I had to take care of myself. I had a great deal of freedom, peppered with the right number of values and responsibilities to keep me in tow. I knew boundaries well and never took advantage of them. But within my boundaries. I had lots of freedom. I enjoyed that feeling of freedom.

I was born in Paris, France, in 1953 and grew up in Louisville, Kentucky, from the age of two till fourteen. Nice southern town. I have lovely memories of growing up within a warm family with loving and caring parents, who were not around during the day because they had to work. It was a given, and I understood that, sort of like not having money for the piano lessons and the piano. I can't say I wasn't lonely sometimes, but it was something I just accepted. I had a lot of time to think, be creative, play, and explore. I already enjoyed my world of art. Another one of my favorite worlds was the local library.

When I was twelve, I saw a movie on TV, *The Diary of Anne Frank*. I was infatuated with it. I can't remember if I really understood what this movie was really about, but I do remember that I was very moved by Anne's story. I ran to the library, got the book, and devoured it. I identified with Anne. We were similar in age. I felt we looked alike, she was Jewish, and I hadn't read any books before about someone Jewish. I lived in the South. Not a lot of stories about Jews down South. She introduced me to a world that I knew existed but that we didn't really talk about in our house. This was a different world of hiding, war, and first love. Hers was my first love story. I was infatuated by this book. I started writing my own diary.

Day 4

The Diary of Anne Frank became a part of me. I was very curious. I think I sort of knew my parents were survivors, but we never really talked about it. I didn't have any living grandparents. My father's parents and my mother's father died in the Holocaust. My mother's mother died when I was two, and then we moved to America. Most of my father's brothers, sisters, and their families died in the war. All the old pictures my parents had of all these relatives fascinated me.

My father had one surviving sister, who moved with her husband and daughter from Paris to Louisville six months after we did. They also would have only one child. She was six months younger than I was. She would be the closest I would ever get to having a sibling. She had beautiful long hair and fancy dresses. I had short hair and I was a tomboy.

My aunt and uncle were also survivors. I don't know how my uncle survived. My aunt was in Auschwitz and had a number. I don't remember when I really started asking questions. But again, we never really talked about it much. I think my father would answer some of my inquiries. But I was never really able to talk to my mother about this. It was too painful for her. I got the idea at a very young age that it was not good to cause my parents pain. They had suffered enough. I was going to be a good girl.

My father had an older surviving brother, Shani, who lived in Israel with his second wife, Ilanka. I can't remember when I first saw the pictures of Shani's first wife and his two beautiful children, Esther and Moshe. They were a beautiful family. I can't remember how old I was when I first heard the terrible tragedy of their death in Auschwitz.

When they arrived in Auschwitz there was a selection. My uncle went to the right. His wife and children went to the left. The little girl tried to run after her father, and a soldier picked her up by the legs and smashed her into a wall, crushing her skull. The little boy ran after the sister and was shot in the head. I can't remember being told that Shani saw it all. I can't remember when I was first told this story and when it became engraved onto my soul. But engraved it is. Another childhood memory.

Day 5

I have good memories of growing up in Kentucky. By day, my father was a kosher butcher, my mother worked in a factory, and I went to school. But the evenings and weekends were ours. I was very much part of their world, as they were part of mine. They would take me everywhere with them, vacations, movies, shopping. We just fit together.

Our home was full of warmth, a home open to everyone. An Orthodox home full of tradition, *Shabbat* candles, *Shabbat* meals with guests, songs, going to synagogues weekly, and wonderful holidays. My father had an open door policy. Living in the South, there weren't a lot of kosher places for visitors and strangers to eat a home-cooked kosher meal. Being the extravert he is, my father would invite people who were passing through and needed a kosher meal or a warm place to stay overnight or for *Shabbat*. There were soldiers from Fort Knox and visitors from Israel.

My father was deeply committed to being religious. His deep commitment to Judaism helped him survive the war, and that same commitment helped him raise a family. I am convinced that my parent's deep commitment was successfully transferred to me. This is what has given me the strong base to raise our family.

My father has a close friend named Mike, close in age to my father, who had survived the war without any family. He never married or had any children. We were Mike's only family. He became very successful financially. Many, many years ago, while my parents were trying to make ends meet, and my father was working six days a week in his butcher business, Mike had asked my father to go into business with him. Mike was not observant, and this meant my father would have had to work on the Sabbath with him. Deeply committed to his faith, devout, and observant, my father refused to go into business with him. This truly was a sacrifice, financially, but he would not sacrifice his beliefs now that he was in a free country and could practice those beliefs freely.

I have found great strength and comfort in my parents' religious observance. Now, all these years later, Mike just celebrated his eighty-fifth birthday. I am sad knowing he is still alone.

Day 6—August 28, 2000

My life is overflowing with the excitement of the daily routine of raising a family, working, and being area coordinator of leaders for La Leche League International in Israel. LLLI is an international organization that offers information and support to women who want to breastfeed their babies. There is no time to write.

In Kentucky, I have fond memories of a family named the Sturmans. Shelly Sturman was my best friend from age ten to fourteen. She came well equipped with the all-American family: two American-born parents, three sisters, an African

American maid who made us wonderful breakfasts, a dog, and a big two-story corner brick house (complete with attic, basement, den with TV, formal dining room, etc.). We were inseparable. I spent a lot of time at her house and many weekends with her. No European accents in this house. It was all-American apple pie. I can still call forth the scent of the house, the warmth of her parents, the rivalry of her siblings. These memories bring inner warmth and a smile to my face.

I went to the local Jewish day school from kindergarten through sixth grade, half-day English studies, half-day Hebrew. The school ended at the sixth-grade level. For seventh and eighth grade I went to the public junior high school. I had lots of friends, both Jewish and not. My parents were okay with that. What became difficult for them was when I began asking questions like, why can't I go to the Friday night parties and be like everyone else? The combination of starting to ask a lot of questions and becoming an adolescent encouraged my parents to start looking for other religious schools for me. The other alternatives meant my going to high school a few hundred miles away from home and living away from home. My parents had one child, and they weren't quite ready for that. After twelve years of hard work and establishing roots, they decided to move to a new city so that I could receive a Jewish high school education. This meant selling everything and starting over from scratch, almost like when they moved from Europe.

Day 7—September 8, 2000

We moved to Los Angeles, California, when I was fourteen years old. Being an adolescent, having to leave all my friends and move to a new community, was very difficult for me. I was very angry and I made life very unpleasant for my parents and myself. I couldn't appreciate the total dedication and devotion they had to Judaism and to what limits they would strive to help insure that I was given a strong Orthodox upbringing. This was truly a sacrifice on their part, to give up everything they had worked so hard to achieve and started to realize in their life in Kentucky.

Starting over is hard for anybody. But for survivors, who have had their childhood, families, and homes stolen, establishing roots is a top priority. The last thing a survivor wants to do is start all over. But now I can appreciate the strong devotion my parents have to their deep belief in God and being observant. The Holocaust will always be a part of them. What happened to them altered their lives forever. But their main connection to Judaism is living an observant Jewish life, and passing on that inheritance to their child and grandchildren.

Their devotion to Judaism had been my guiding light. With this same kind of devotion, my husband, Ron, and I have been able to follow our dream of raising our sons in Israel for the past seventeen years. Our beliefs have given an almost exhilarating atmosphere to our family. Ron and I are a team, a very volatile team. We have been together for thirty-one years (twenty-seven married). We are moving now into a new phase of our marriage where we are witnessing the rewards of our twenty-four years of parenting. Watching the small miracles of God in our everyday life mixed into the countless hours of hard work. Watching our children grow into young adults, learning Torah, finding jobs, making commitments, and passing on the strong traditions and love for Judaism that have been ingrained so tenderly into their lives.

So you see, Hitler didn't succeed in his goal of wiping us out. We are here, and we are even stronger. Living a life full of tradition and joy. Raising the next generation in our country, *Eretz Yisrael.* There are scars, anger, and pain, but they are not our focus. Not for my parents, not for me, not my children.

At the age of seventy-nine and sixty-eight, my parents made *aliyah* in 1999, after living in Los Angeles for thirty-two years. To this day they practice a commitment to their religion and ideals, ideals that helped them survive the Holocaust, pick up the pieces, and raise another generation. These are the exhilarating moments that fill our lives with strength, courage, and continued commitment to our faith and our country.

ROSIE WEISEL was born in Paris, France, but her family emigrated to America when she was young. She was raised in Kentucky and California but has lived on Kibbutz Saad for the past seven years. The mother of six sons: Adir, Raphael, Gavrieal, Chanan, Yididya, and Tzur, Ms. Weisel has been a graphic artist and calligrapher for 26 years and has designed and written illuminated manuscripts and family trees. She has been a Le Leche League leader (an international breastfeeding organization) for twenty-two years. For the past four, she has taken care of young children on the kibbutz where she and her family are permanent residents.

Nava Semel and her mother.

To my mother, who showed me the light through the glass.
To my father, who taught me how to embrace the past.
They always hold my trembling hand when I write.

Shirley Barenholz, a Dutch/Israeli photographer and a daughter of a Holocaust survivor from Bergen Belsen, published *Children of Hope* in Holland in 1998. This book follows with photos and text on the lives of twelve Israeli families, whose older parent survived the horror and began a new hopeful chapter in Israel. The thirteenth chapter is about the author herself living in Holland.

Chapter 10

A HAT OF GLASS

Nava Semel

Nava Semel is one of Israel's finest contemporary writers, and one of the first Israeli women to address the Holocaust in fiction and prose. Proud of her parents' survival and determined not to let the memories die, she has become the voice for the second generation through her work. When I met her in Israel for the first time, in the spring of 2000, I felt that we had known each other our entire lives. —MW

This is not the whole truth. Just bits and pieces of it sloughed off over the passing years. As I gather them up, they seem at times like crumbs from bread that's turned moldy. Whenever I've tried to see the whole of it with my own eyes, it's been like walking backwards. I take care not to bump into the wall behind me. It's an ache I've known before.

"Clarissa," I called after her in the street.

I think about her sometimes. Never actually forget her.

I started running after her, but stopped. She'd become no more than a speck of gray that kept getting smaller and smaller. As I watched, something turned inside me, then turned again and again, until it reached all the way back to the way things had been at the beginning.

It was three months before the end of the war, but we didn't know it yet. I had no recollection of my face, hardly remembered my age either. I had no way of knowing that the man I'd married three years earlier and had lived with in western Hungary had been consumed by then in a cloud of smoke.

Nor could I conjure up the dead fetus I'd been carrying inside me for two whole months—the soundless, motionless load that left no trace save a hidden line curving its way across my stomach. The body was one I hadn't seen in all those years since the war began. Even the menstrual blood, dependable as the seasons, the blood that might have assured me that at a time like this the sun was still revolving on its axis and that the universe was following its usual course, it, too, was taken away from me.

Janine, the French girl, said they were adding some sort of potion to the watered-down liquid they used to shove at us, announcing: "Soup." Except that for me, to know that the bleeding had stopped was undeniable proof that time had frozen, and that something was guarding the straits, lest even the slightest rush of hot dust push its way through and dissipate the heavy slumber. Those who had been consumed through the chimneys were the only ones to rise away, to beg for mercy.

In the long line that shuffled through each morning, only one thought kept flickering in my mind. I longed to spot those bombers in the sky zeroing in on the cursed spot and wiping it away, the same as you wipe away a spot of blood after being struck across the mouth, then wipe it away again, until the only traces are the small drops on your hand, not a sign of it remaining on your mouth. But the wound kept oozing, and there was nobody to rise up and put a curse on the place, to make certain that nothing ever grew there again.

When my son went to see it, only one generation later, he returned heavy-hearted and told me: "Mother, the ground is covered over with grass."

I asked myself what kind of a short memory the Creator must have, to be so good to that soil and not to have damned it. Planting a seed in it, no less, never felling its grass. He may go so far as to add some flowers just to please it. Can't He even bide his time until those of us who cursed it are no longer here to watch?

It was my last *selektion*. Who knows, perhaps the face unwittingly etched on me by my father and mother was what had kept me alive. Even now, when I study the rounded lines that frame my children's faces, I wonder whether that was what made me seem healthy enough, still fit.

Five hundred of us they chose, and took us to the sealed railway car. The doors were bolted and just beyond them we could hear the horror-stricken voices of those not chosen.

"Don't go near the door," the *Kapo* said. "They're finishing off the ones left behind."

Then they hitched the car to the back of the train. For four days we traveled, us chosen girls, our bodies deep in excrement and degradation. The stench was polluting the planet like the detritus of giants, bound to fall like ripe fruit and be utterly shattered. A few loaves of bread tossed inside just a moment before the train pulled away represented the innermost wish of someone hoping to buy us a little more time. Between the slats in the sides you could catch a glimpse of the earth moving. Were we going around in circles, only to wind up back where we'd started? The passing of time was marked by the jerking of our bodies packed together like worms, coupled with the relentless churning of the wheels as they thrust us forward along overworked tracks.

Many hours later the train stopped. Its doors opened suddenly, but instead of daylight, we saw the dusk of evening. A rush of cool November air clashed with the stench. That was when it hit me full force, as palpably as when a cripple fingers his deformity, only to be overcome by excruciating shame. We stood there in the big station, and the darkness cringed before the ray of light along the tracks. Trembling, we stood, exhausted from the trip, our rags clinging to our bodies, enveloped in stench. I had no idea what phantom world they'd brought us to and where they'd be hustling us to next. The end was near, but we didn't know it. A man stepped out of the darkness and started in our direction. He was tall and his white locks glistened as they fell neatly over his forehead and temples. He was wearing a *Wehrmacht* uniform without the SS skull and crossbones. Five hundred pairs of eyes looked at him in mute terror. I heard a sigh, but it may have been my imagination. His face was clearly visible in the light of the emerging moon. Incredulous at first, he soon turned his head away in disgust. Later I saw the sorrow, too; he could not wipe it away.

"Women," he muttered and his face cut through our tightness. "You've arrived at a labor camp. You are in Germany and this is Zittau."

There was a wrenching moan of anguish. He came a step closer, and the front row of women moved back, pushing back the ones behind. He held out his arm.

"You women have nothing to be afraid of. Nobody is going to harm you here. This is a labor camp."

We'd heard about those by now. We'd already been in another camp. I couldn't believe it. The old man in his elegant uniform did not conceal the surge of compassion that swept him at the sight of the tortured creatures before him. He took another step and touched one of the women standing near him, then fingered the frayed edge of her dress.

"It's a disgrace," he said. "It's a disgrace to look this way. *Das ist eine grosse Schande.*" He brought his palms together. "Women," he said again, "I was an officer in the Great War. You were brought into the *Reich* in order to work in the factories here." With a flourish, he motioned toward the large barracks whose silhouettes stood out against the darkness.

"So long as I am here and you apply yourselves to your work, nobody will harm you. I give you my word—the word of an officer who fought in the Great War."

Then he turned on his heel and hurried off, disappearing in the darkness.

"It's a disgrace," he had said.

We're nothing more than a crisscrossing shadow, a huddle of humanity with a flimsy breath of life still flickering inside us. The old officer was not with us long. Some SS women assigned to guard us let it be known that he was too soft, and that the surge of pity had been his downfall.

I don't know what they did with him. A solitary ray of light had touched the darkness, only to be extinguished. The self-same darkness was free to reassert its haughty sway over a locked planet. We are still no more than prey, I told myself, still not members of the human race.

At four-thirty, with the morning still reluctant to unfold, we rise. Treading gingerly, we make our way to the washroom at the end of the corridor. Shaven scalps bend over the basins. Every time I bring water to my mouth, it works its way into the spaces where I once had the shiny, white teeth of a young girl. When they took me from my home, the Nazi struck me, and during those first few hours, fragments of teeth kept rolling about inside my mouth. I could neither spit them out nor swallow them. All I drank was my blood, and its taste was peculiar.

At five, the kitchen workers haul in a large pot, holding it by both handles and dragging it along the floor. One at a time, we fill our dishes and sip the murky liquid in short gulps. It has neither smell nor taste, and only the heat of it reaches our bodies. We'd stand there, in rows of five, in the doorway, pressed up against each other, huddling tightly to keep warm. The prisoners' uniforms hung loosely on our bodies, and the stripes outlined our emaciated forms. Over our shriveled breasts, there was a gray stripe with our badge, the yellow Star of David, on it, and a number. Even in the darkness it lost none of its shine. Two, nine, six, three, four.

"Who are you? Who are you?" "I don't know. I don't remember."

I would recite my number over and over again, like a dybbuk slipping out of its bottle, then back in again.

We stand there tensely, side by side, in frozen anticipation. At a quarter to six we hear the sound of footsteps—master of the women. What an icy expression God has given him. Never a twitch. Nothing ever fluttered or glinted. He would flash a look in our direction as though seeing the scum of the earth. Marching behind him was his bevy of women officers, his chorus, in their spotless uniforms and shining boots, taking count. Day after day, the same count. Next, one of them would tour the rooms, inspect the pallets, and depart. Then he would move on. Sometimes he would crack his whip; he'd never use his open palm. The very touch might be infectious. The overseer's entourage included one golden-haired officer, Brunhild of the Black Forest. Utterly untarnished, without so much as a furrow near her eyes or cheeks. Only the slightest rosiness, as if to say, how healthy I am, O noble beauty.

The rows extended as far as the eye could see in either direction, and the only sound was that of plodding footsteps. The women's arms drooped like two extra stripes, like flaccid worms.

In the large workshops, along the workbenches, were the airplane parts for us to polish with whetstones and wheels and assorted implements whose exact nature baffled me. Nor did I know just how to fit them together. And in my dreams I again find myself holding a shiny metallic object and struggling to fit it back where it belongs, but it resists. I try to force, it but it refuses. Until suddenly it dissolves and the molten steel slithers across my fingers and up my stripes, reaching the back of my neck, where it settles, trying to strangle me.

She hardly says anything. Only the bare essentials. Mingling among us and watching. A broad-framed woman, she wears a prisoner's uniform like the rest of us, but she's different. Imprisonment hasn't clung to her.

Janine the Frenchwoman, whose pallet is next to mine, says: "This Clarissa was a *fronthure*."

I tell my children that she was a whore sent as a diversion for the soldiers more than three years earlier. Several others like her had already thrown themselves against the fence to sever the frenzied memories. Others had turned into wild dogs, directing their humiliation and disgrace at women as yet unafflicted.

But not Clarissa. The way I remember it, the torment never took hold of her.

Day follows day in confusion. There's no keeping track. One morning I awake on my pallet, but it feels like smoldering stones. There I am in a vast desert, the furnace overhead sapping whatever precious fluids still flow inside me. I implore it to take even more.

Janine drags me off the cot. "Get up," she says, almost shouting. I don't budge. The goodness of the desert is what I want. She prods me, but I can't move my legs. They're drowning in the desert sands and I haven't the will. Janine beats me with her fists.

"On your feet," she says, "or you'll be missed in the roll call. You mustn't be sick!" she shouts. "Mon dieu, you just can't take that kind of risk."

"Leave me alone," I beg of her. Janine persists and forces my feet toward her, tying my shoes on.

And above, out of the fiery skies, comes a different voice. "Leave her alone!" Janine pounces on her.

"Monster," she yells. "She'll die if she doesn't get up!"

The vast desert drifts away. I open my eyes, which feel like tiny flames. Like from days gone by, Clarissa's voice lacks the parched sound that comes from unremitting hunger and a wilting mind.

"You fool," she says to Janine. "You know I wouldn't let her die. Just leave her here." Bowing to Clarissa's authority, Janine loosens her stubborn grip.

"Now leave," she orders.

Clarissa kneels and takes off my shoes. She lifts my spindly legs back onto the cot.

"I'll be back soon," she whispers.

I don't know where she went but she did come back, and in the hollow of her palm were some tablets, gleaming. A kind I had never seen here. Perhaps she's out to poison me, to embed her evil in me, to scar me with her shame. But I keep still. Like an obedient child, I open my mouth and swallow. Into another desert I sink. There's the hint of a breeze brushing its precious sands, stirring up pillars of dust.

For three days she keeps coming, putting the medication in my mouth, and disappearing. On the fourth day, as Janine tells it, Clarissa stood during the first roll call at the end of the corridor and waited. Then, when the golden-haired officer arrived, Clarissa stopped her and whispered something in her ear. The officer approached her master and he took the roll call, but not a single woman was missing.

I was not the only one of whom Clarissa took charge at a harrowing moment. There were others like me. She brought medicine to the ailing, solace to the dying, wetting their foreheads with soothing compresses until the end.

For Sarah Mendelssohn, who came down with the sailors' disease, scurvy, she brought fruits and vegetables.

The only islands of potatoes we ever saw floating in the lake of soup appeared on those rare days when the factory owners came to see the prisoners. That was how we found out about the orders to give us more and better food to make us more productive. But the SS men would fish any morsels of vegetable and shreds of meat out of the soup, leaving us nothing but the greasy water, without a trace of the nourishment it once contained.

When I tried to thank her, haltingly, she brushed me aside with a flick of her hand and turned away, as though it was more than she could bear.

Late one night, the door came open quietly. Clarissa got up and walked toward it, treading very carefully, as if on sizzling embers. She made her way to the pale slit of light, and as the door opened wider, I could make out the shadow of the golden-haired officer. She was standing there blocking the light. As soon as Clarissa crossed the threshold, the officer turned on her heel and Clarissa followed. The door closed silently, as though it had never moved. I fasten my head to the hardness of the pallet, and as I turn back, I find Janine's eyes, like a cat's, slicing through me in the darkness. I turn away. The silence hangs so heavy that I can almost hear the Frenchwoman's eyelids batting, and the sound of my own breathing rumbles in my ears.

Other nights she stayed awake altogether. We knew well enough where sleep would overtake her. Nestling in the embrace of the woman officer, her gateway to the world. Sometimes, she would be allowed to hear a Chopin polonaise or a Wagner symphony. To rest her back against the crisp sheets. And the Brunhild would offer her soft clothes, wash her body in a tub, shampoo her hair. Clarissa would lie there with her legs curled up and her mind closed within itself. At the morning parade, a telltale nerve would twitch in the officer's cheek as she passed by Clarissa.

Clarissa never said much while she worked, but once she started singing in a deep, low voice, like a husky gurgle. She fought back the strange sound but it kept pouring out of her, unchecked, spilling on to our workbenches.

Unable to continue joining the airplane parts with that terrible sound, we stopped. It was like a mute, straining to use his voice, the tremor of his vocal cords causing his listeners to shudder.

One night I awoke and found that Clarissa had returned to her cot from the hidden room. But instead of stretching out, she was sitting there like a statue in whom life had frozen, staring out into the darkness.

I could not stop myself from going over to her.

"Clarissa." I spoke softly, "What does she do to you?" Suddenly her face contorted with a pain so intense that I recoiled. She turned her head slowly, as though a key had been inserted in her back, and said dryly: "She doesn't do me any harm." Then she touched my head.

"You're young," she said.

"Why, I almost had a child, and my youth is gone."

"You'll have other children." She touches my forehead. "I never will."

Once a fate is sealed, wherever the body goes, that fate precedes it. People shy away as they would from someone with a dreaded disease, but the body has its own truth to tell. It follows its course, spinning and stumbling, never to be shaken off. She has been branded and the stigma can never be shaken off. She has been branded and the stigma can never be wiped away. Clearly, she will never be free to love again, as we will if ever we get out. The bruises and emaciation, the disease and the wounds have gnawed away at the racked bodies, but though they are torn, they will be given another chance. Like a forest that goes on burning after a fire. The soft murmur of the sea at high tide and the waves of the moon will bring other loves and children into those wombs. Beyond the vastness of this nightmare, we will rediscover love. There will we give birth and raise our children. Not on bread but on water. Not on the body but on the scarred soul. This scarred soul of mine opens up to her, longing for her support. But she has already been branded. For the rest of her life she will wander through the Land of Nod, with no brave hunter to go with her. Nothing but her seared spirit.

Softly I ask, since she is the one who knows: "Will we ever get out of here?" She says, "They're getting closer. It won't be long before the echoes of the explosions reach us."

She bends over me and shares her secret. "I'll be going to Palestine. I have an uncle there, my mother's brother. We used to make fun of him. We said he was crazy going to such a god-forsaken place. But here I am now, without any God. I'll join him. He's an important man by now in Palestine." She utters the word gently, splitting the name of the country, syllable by euphonious syllable, before her voice drops to where it becomes eerie and remote.

Clarissa rocks herself as though in a lullaby. She's far away from me by now, and we're like moles in a tunnel, except that we haven't had the welcome sleep those wise animals have. All we've done is crawl down into the deepest holes where the abomination flows submissively, begging to pour out to sea. But the sea is thousands of miles away over occupied land. The roots of the burning trees tremble and cower under the weight of the abomination, demanding to know where the water will come from. Every last one of the bridges has been bombed this winter, yet the trains have not stopped crossing the rivers. People have become roots and roots, people. The wise animals listen to the sound of the flowing abomination and wonder when it will let up.

I can't go any closer to her. I return to my cot, as she goes on rocking herself, consoling her flesh and her spirit, no longer taking any notice of me.

Winter was digging in around us and we were forgotten. Heavy rains started to fall, and it seemed to me that every drop was also carrying a grain of ashes from those consumed by the smoke. The camp was not bombed, but the approaches were covered in marshy mud, as the trudging of the sticky feet and the sheer fatigue kept beating, like the room of a watchmaker gone berserk. Whenever I caught a glimpse beyond the fences, I would see the treetops swaying in the forest.

It was there that the leaves would fill up with drops of water and the early winter winds would smooth over the rows of foliage. Some of the leaves reached over the fence and even drifted down into the doorways of the barracks.

These were left untouched. Except by the wind, which, after all, was good to them.

New airplane parts were piled high on the workbenches, and we fitted them together helplessly. The door opened and Clarissa entered, wearing a pair of men's boots. Water dripped off them onto the floor, leaving the tracks of her hurried entrance.

Out of the coat wrapped around her, she took a kerchief and unfolded it, revealing the shiny redness of forest berries. She opened her mouth and flicked in one berry, then another. The juice oozed down her chin like a festering wound. The *meisters*, the German mechanics appointed to guard over us during working hours, stopped what they were doing and watched. We all huddled around her as she began stuffing our hands and our mouths with ripe, red berries. My mother's jars are brimming with red jam, and she lines them up, one by one, on the pantry shelves for all the seasons to come until the following summer.

"Where did you get them?" one woman asked.

"It's a present," said Clarissa breaking into a raucous laugh and swaying from side to side. "I'm kept as a lover, didn't you know?"

Then she pressed her head into the empty kerchief and breathed in the lingering fragrance of the fruit. The kerchief covered her, but we could still see the shivers running down her spine. We left her there in her kerchief. Not a single one of us touched her. We went back to our workbenches and clung to them. Even the *meisters* left her alone, until the door opened again. In the doorway was the officer, some loose strands of golden hair dangling under her hat and falling damply along her neck. She went over to Clarissa, took her by the shoulders and shook her with one powerful jolt. The kerchief dropped to the ground, the red spots embedded in it. Then she bent over and picked it up. It was the first time I had seen her bend over. Her spine jutted out under the blouse of her uniform and we could follow her breathing. The sight of her stunned me. A tremendous revelation. Even she, proud as she was, knew how to bend. The taut cord that had learned how to stretch, never allowing itself to slacken, had loosened ever so briefly. So she is no different from the rest of us.

"*Das ist meine Clarissa,*" she said in a stiff voice. "*Sie ist Mein.*"

"Mine, mine."

As she straightened up, the kerchief dropped again and she stepped on it. We turned around. Janine was the only one who dared. She took one step forward, shooting out a piercing look, the officer directly across from her.

For a split second their eyes met, a moment that froze in space. The officer turned, let go of Clarissa, and Clarissa stumbled. Where is Janine? A Catholic who had coupled her fate with a Jew. Following him eastward. That's how she wound up with us. Where is Janine now? In some vinegrowers' village near Montpellier, not far from the Spanish border, where the grapes are unusually juicy, where one can get as drunk on a single bunch of them as on a flask of wine.

I am not yet sixty. I took my granddaughter Hagar to the house from which they removed me.

I could not tell the ten-year-old that this was where I had loved another man. There had been a fetus inside me who might have become her father. I told her.

"This is where I once lived. This is where they banged on my door. This was where they dragged us outside and took us to the town square."

Hagar looked wistfully at the house we had not entered and asked: "Why don't you knock on the door, Grandmother?"

I said to myself: that door has been slammed shut for good. It can't be reopened. Deep in the recesses of my memory I buried that man who had slept in my bed and was the first to come to me. I don't dream about him anymore. When Hagar's grandfather took me, I cast that chapter of my life aside into a sealed box and threw the key into the depths of the sea. Still, it is beyond me how these things seep through and gather in other parts of me, filtering into my children.

The dammed-up waters seek new outlets. When I heard them forcing their way, I clasped my head with both hands and ordered: "Stop!" But they disobeyed. Outsmarting me, they worked their way in between the cracks.

I clasped my granddaughter's hand and felt its fervor. She was standing next to me, so keen and pure. I said to myself: I'm not trying to get even. I'll be sixty next year, after all. I've brought along my son's daughter, to show the intruders who broke the door down—those masters of the stripes and the whip—that they haven't outdone me.

The fetus died, but here is the child.

Winter was coming and the sun had almost vanished. The rumble of distant explosions blended with the sound of thunder. Nothing but the lightning, slashing the clouds, could keep them apart.

A few weeks before liberation, the *meisters* began shooting indiscriminately. People disappeared from the factories and the owners vanished. A day before the liberation, we remained all alone in the camp.

We woke up in the chilly dawn and stood in formation waiting, but there were no footsteps to be heard. We ventured out into the gateways of the barracks. Everything was in place. The fences were bolted. In the distance, the treetops were swaying as though nothing in the forest had changed. Utterly indifferent to us, it had never turned a receptive ear. By noon, the gate had been uprooted. Two dogs still posted to watch over it were shot on the spot, and their carcasses left to rot.

A Russian division arrived in the camp and our fears gave way to new ones. Fresh from the battles of Stalingrad, they would be overcome by cold and lust. But as soon as they saw us, they turned away. Our emaciated bodies were powerless to stir any passion.

We lined up for the last time, facing the row of Russian officers who wished to provide us with the first piece of paper we would need to begin life anew. They gave us back our names. I saw mine, but we were strangers to one another.

Janine said it amounted to a baptism and kept crossing herself. Three Russian officers sat at a desk taken from the camp headquarters. I remembered the second chapter. God takes the finest rib, the one that has suffered nightmares, and releases it in the Garden.

Clarissa's icy hand was tugging at mine, the way it did that time when she handed me the medicine.

I turned toward her and she pointed wordlessly at a woman who was working her way into the waiting row. She had taken on our appearance, turned into one of us. Got hold of a striped shirt, hoping to find refuge in our fold. Gone was Brunhild's golden hair. She had shaven it all off and her skull bones were showing. All that time, they had been covered by the flowing Brunhildian mane. The color was gone from her cheeks, and her anxiety was seeping out, as if through a faulty stopper. I looked and saw her. She had pushed her way into the hush of the women and, even from as far away as I was standing, I could see the roundness of her breasts between the stripes. She'd been cut off like us. Now she was hoping for the final Judgment Day. The trumpets of angels.

"Oh, merciful Christ," said Janine, stretching out an arm in her direction. Then she spit on the ground and made the sign of the cross.

Thus in the haze of my illness she reemerges out of the ground in her striped uniform. Her hair falls on her shoulders and the SS insignia is etched in blood on her forehead. Even in my nightmares she bears that same deathly pallor. She leans over me, opens her fist, and shows me some yellow tablets.

I yell: "I'm not to blame!" She grabs me and forces them into my mouth. I purse my lips, seal them tight, and cry:

"Clarissa, help me!"

But it's my husband who shakes me by the shoulder and asks: "What's wrong? You've been having a nightmare."

One morning he asked me: "Who is the Clarissa you keep dreaming about?"

She keeps surfacing. Weaving in and out of the corridors of my memory. Pulling behind the dignity of man and his degradation, his anguish, and his powers of resistance. The eyes of Janine of Gaul harden as she struggles to record what she sees, indelibly, to make sure that she never forgets. Clarissa had said: "I can't be the one to turn her in." "You go," she told me. "Go tell the Russians that she's hiding among us." I froze. My legs wouldn't move. I was unable to shout. I remembered the outstretched palm and the tablets. But Janine had already stepped out of the line and her legs were carrying her unhaltingly, overcome by some secret power. She approached the Russian officers and told them something. Two of them followed her back. Ever so slowly, they approached us.

Janine stood opposite the Nazi and pointed her out with an arched hand. "That's the one!" The officers dragged her away and the Brunhild started screaming and jerking convulsively. But the Russian had a firm grip on her. He made her stand up as he struck her on her bald pate. That was how I was later able to picture her skull lying there on the ground after the worms had had their fill. He wasted no time, pulling at her shirt, ripping it right off. She began screaming again and covered her nakedness with her hands. But those breasts were not like ours. Full and fleshy they cut through the torn material.

He slapped her once across the face and she stopped. Her arms fell to her sides. He raised her arm for all to see. Under it was the mark, carefully etched, as though on a sheet of paper. Furiously he struck her again. She lifted her head and searched over the entire row of women until her eyes rested on Clarissa.

Clarissa turned away, no longer seeing her. Like a madwoman she screeched, her cries rising and falling over our frozen silence. "Clarissa, help me!" The Russian waited another minute, then dragged her away. She stopped screaming and he pulled her behind him like a tattered sack, behind the first barracks.

A single gunshot and he was back. As he stuck his pistol back in its holster as if nothing had happened, he returned to his seat by the desk. I turned to look into the row of women, but Clarissa wasn't there. She had vanished. I shut my eyes. The entire row turned into one long strip, and at the tip of the worm, one after the other, we undressed and put on the clothes provided by the Russians.

Ever since those sinister days, the light for me will forever be flawed.

When I returned home, I found my parents alive. For three days, my again father sat with me. Then he packed a small bag. I asked him: "Why are you leaving now that I've been saved?"

For two months he traveled all over Europe to collect the proof we would need for me to be able to remarry. "The only way to find the necessary two witnesses," he explained, "is to start searching right away. If we wait, they'll scatter all over the world, and we will never be able to prove you're a widow." My children are grown, and the dead one who dropped out of my womb is over and done with. The ones who followed covered over it with their beauty and brightness.

I once took out a picture of my dead husband to show my oldest son, but he didn't believe me. The truth, after all, is a great mosaic, with new pieces forever falling into place. When one piece is missing, sometimes I look for it and sometimes I stop.

Whenever I pass by the road signs of our country, I think about her. Maybe she is here, maybe there. Maybe her face is sealed, revealing nothing, except for the wet and oozing sap of berries.

Whenever I dare to lift the stone, I turn it over and over, and things are not the way they were before, but rather the way one sees them in a crooked mirror or through a window on a foggy day. I'm not about to breathe warm mist onto the pane, because I don't really want to see Clarissa in a golden embrace, and Janine with the vinegrowers of Gaul, and myself in Tel Aviv. Only rarely does my soul wander and turn over, but it no longer reaches back to the way things had been at the beginning.

The way that time adds layers of its own and that you cannot reach back to the day of Creation without climbing down a great canyon. After passing all seven layers of the earth, one moves back a million years, to the Day of Chaos when Creation and Disintegration were one, nesting in a single womb, like Rebecca's irreconcilable twins.

There, a great darkness emerged. They say time heals. They say I will be healed. I am grateful for the sun and for the new light, but on the heads of my children, my anguish and torment sit like a hat of glass.

NAVA SEMEL, born in Tel Aviv, is the author of five books and two plays. Her work highlights the second generation of Holocaust survivors in Israel. She is the recipient of numerous awards, including the 1991 National Jewish Book Award for *Becoming Gershona*.

Zdenka and Marek Morsel, Czechoslovakia, 1938

For my parents

Chapter 11

FRAGMENTS AND WHISPERS

Miriam Morsel Nathan

Miriam Morsel Nathan's poetry is deeply visual. Miriam captures the flavors, colors, textures, sounds, and fragrances of Europe before and during the war. I am always amazed how one word of her poetry can contain a volume of life. My dear Miriam, the poet. —MW

I am a poet, and my work reflects a history I inherited, but did not live; a memory of experiences and loss I absorbed but did not have. My work is infused with European sensibility, images, culture, and iconography of a particular time in an endless search for the past and a constant sense of the contrasting present.

My mother, Zdenka Schwarz Morsel, was born in a small town outside of Prague called Pribram. My father, Marek Morsel, came from Orlova, also a small town, in Silesia, which was Czech, Austro-Hungarian, or Polish, depending on the borders at any particular time. After my parents married in 1937, they lived in Prague.

In 1939, my father began an odyssey through Yugoslavia, Greece, and Italy and eventually left Europe illegally, headed for the United States. He was stranded on Ellis Island for four months until the Hebrew Immigrant Aid Society offered him the opportunity to go to the Dominican Republic, where President Rafael Trujillo had created a safe haven—an agricultural settlement for the Jews—called Sosua. My father became one of the first settlers of Sosua; he was a farmer, then an importer/exporter. He later moved to the capital city, Santo Domingo (then known as Cuidad Trujillo), where he lived throughout the war years.

My mother was unable to get exit papers to leave Europe, so she remained in Prague, working illegally, until she was deported to Terezin, with her father, on July 23, 1942. She had exceptional stenography and typing skills, in both German and Czech, and became very useful in the central office of Terezin, where she worked the night shift, typing the lists of names of individuals to be transported to the east. My mother remained in Terezin until she was liberated in 1945. My father's parents, two sisters, two brothers-in-law, nephew, and his brother's wife and daughter perished in Auschwitz. My mother's two brothers were sent east. One was shot in a mass execution, the other perished in Dachau. My mother's father died of dysentery in Terezin. In 1946, my mother joined my father in the Dominican Republic, and I was born there in 1947.

I live my life in the present, a contemporary woman with a family, a profession, and an unyielding sensuous enchantment with the world. I gravitate toward a kind of surrealism in my work and allow my senses to be my interpreter as I write of lost people, another time and place, shadows and grief. I fuse the tangible objects and recollections I keep from my childhood with those stories heard in fragments and whispers, those ephemeral pieces of my history and of those people whose photos fill the old brown leather box in my parents' closet—people who look like me, laughing in the sun, standing by lakes, in the mountains, walking, arms linked, with lovers or friends on cobblestone streets, whose faces I know, but whom I've never met, people who did not return, but who live in my poetry.

In Berlin

Through a neon tunnel
of pink yellow light
a woman emerges and
steps off the curb into pouring rain
her black velvet cape skimming
puddles, a rhinestone tiara
making an inverted rain shower of
hot white above her dark hair.
She hurries to a café under the tracks
where the vibrations of trains
shake the wine glasses on tables
swilling garnet liquid against
the hard sides of the crystal.
She can stay only a short while
as she must weave a shroud
before dawn. It will be red because the water
runs red from the faucets, like someone
bleeding into the pipes,
in this city of trains, this city
where mementos of destruction
begging to be forgotten
fit just inside hidden pockets,
cower under black velvet capes,
and leach into rhinestone fingers.

In the House of the Thousand Candles

In the house of the thousand candles
old women pray for the safe return of soldiers
while eating little duck hearts sautéed in butter.

Fig and almond orchards grow in the place
where the sky and earth meet. When their prayers go
    unheeded,
the old women wrap holy stones in white lace-trimmed
    handkerchiefs

and place them inside the coffins of their dead men.
Draped in black, they sit at heavy tables and eat yogurt
    with date honey.
Oddly, there are pink roses in silver pitchers on the mantle.

On days when their prayers are answered
the old women cover their shoulders with small white
    shawls
and light a thousand candles in the windows

overlooking the sea. After dinner they open crimson
    umbrellas,
and walk arm in arm in the black of night.

Berlin Fragments

Platinum hair slicked back
a young waiter in a café
brings me rolls and marmalade.

At the edge of a horizon
an industrial chimney
spits gray smoke...

Stay on the S-Bahn line
No. 1 until the last stop.
It's just a short ride to

Sachsenhausen
OPEN DAILY
from 8:30 A.M. until 4:30 P.M.

Dresden saucers in the window
of a dark antique shop
on a ruler-straight boulevard.

The buses run precisely on time.

Why Marlene Didn't Come Back
to the Fatherland

They say Marlene Dietrich
was married in the Kaiser-Wilhelm Church
which is now a war memorial, half bombed out,
iridescent blue at night. Across the street,
in Berlin's largest department store,
people in scarves and coats sample wursts,
cheeses, and coffee on a February afternoon
in the food emporium on the sixth floor.
I buy slippers for my father in that store,
wondering whose feet have been in them.
The chanteuse, dead now, lies under birch
trees in the Stubenrauchstrasse Cemetery
while her 440 pairs of shoes, 400 hats,
150 pairs of gloves, 300 dresses and suits,
are piled in a brick warehouse
in the Spandau district waiting for cataloging.
They joke there is enough to stock the women's
section of Berlin's largest department store.
The right wing to this day doesn't like her.
They think she sold out to Hollywood,
was a traitor to the Fatherland—though there *are* some
who regularly send sprays of white roses for her grave.
My father says the slippers don't quite fit.
Something on the inside is rubbing a sore.

Memory Interruptus

Roll call and she stood for hours...
with the small pot she found...
wedged between her legs... so later...
she and her sisters...who...because
they were blond and young... were often...
well...so what was it?...
oh yes...so they could boil
the two potatoes...they had hidden
in the wall of the lager...

The Absurd Messiah

It will be in the season
of the magnolia's blossoming.
The messiah will wear
a helmet and biker's spandex
when he arrives holding
in one hand photographs
of someone's dead lovers,
and cupped in the hollow of the other,
the foggy bellow of a French horn.
Two cranes destined for each other
will collide, then part. In a café
on a side street lovers will smoke
cigars and eat black olives with onions.
Women will seduce men
by crying. And then,
after one full year of light,
followed by a hundred of darkness,
a crescent moon will hang backwards
in a night silent as the inside of a violin.

Die Nachtigall

It means *the nightingale* and it's because
he sings not on stage anymore but in cafés
late at night where he makes rounds with his
German songs at his side, pulling off a black
felt hat—his small head with toothless mouth
perched above a checkered scarf—and then
pulls from his pocket old news clippings
from a time when he was young though
he claims still to be less than 31 years old,
this *nachtigall* who has been out of work
for more than one third of his "age," who
sings for his supper and gums a smile
while he moves on to the next café and the next
as young people endlessly smoke cigarettes
and the city quiets down, this *nachtigall*
who flits as if he were moving between
the branches of lilac bushes in the spring
carrying under his thin wings
the tunes of their thousand souls.

The Tattoo Lady

It's a blue blur on her arm
while she reaches
across the table for a fig.
You don't see it at first.
You think your eyes
are playing tricks, that there's
a smudge, must be some ink
from a letter she was writing
to one of her unaccented kids
in some American city.
She reaches over again
and you look hard. And then you see it.
It makes you think maybe
you should drop a note to her kid
and say I saw your mother
and she's OK and I guess
you know this but somehow
she can't get rid of that tattoo.
And then you want to say to that kid,
you must have spent your childhood
trying to rub it off.

Sister Maria Roberta Says the Dead Miss Us and Are Jealous

There's a coffin on the gondola
and the woman going to the funeral
has one hip higher than the other. Her name is
Sister Maria Roberta. Later, over a wooden table,
in the shadow of death and afternoon light,
she fills a white ceramic bowl with pomegranates,
talking of angels. Her favorite is called Pascal.
Sister Maria Roberta talks incessantly and sprinkles
	aromatic ashes
on bread hot from the oven. *One prayer will take away
one hour of fire from hell* she says. Sister Maria Roberta
grinds seeds, and says *death builds its scratchy nest,
and carries under his hairy arm the blue straw of
	our muscles.*
Sister Maria Roberta says that five generations of the dead
attend each wedding and even the blind must bless the
	moon.

Music for Lovers and Then Others

Cosima Wagner woke up one morning
to the sound of a full orchestra in the hallway
at the bottom of the stairs because, for her birthday,
her husband, Richard, had written a symphony.
Richard was not known for such sentimentality.
But for Cosima, the mother of his children,
and from whom he could not be parted,
Richard would do anything. His tenderness to her
masked his passion against things he did not like.
Anarchist, vegetarian, anti-Semite, Richard regarded himself
as the "most German of men" and after tea
each day, played long melodies for Cosima.
When Cosima died it would be twelve years
before someone played Richard's music
as accompaniment to the parting of wives, husbands,
and children in the stained courtyards of Poland.

Lovers and Gravediggers

In exchange for a bed with sheets, nine men,
two of them medical doctors,
hire themselves out as dancers at an elegant
hotel in Italy sometime in 1939. Like lovers,
sporting pencil-thin mustaches and white summer suits,
they lean on the arms of heavily upholstered
chairs in the gilded lobby, waiting for perfumed
women in good leather high heels with thin ankle straps.
But who comes instead is a woman in a brown
form-fitting suit, Persian lamb at the cuffs,
sheer stockings with seams like line drawings
down the center of each leg. She wears
no perfume and is sad: she has come from a funeral
where the gravediggers set up chairs on the muddy
hump of dirt under which her mother is buried.
The woman tells the nine men, two of them medical
     doctors,
how she watched someone sit on her mother's neck
throughout the funeral. One of the lovers
with a pencil-thin mustache begins to cry,
surprised at his own sentimentality.
The woman in brown decides to call him
"my pretty man." They leave together to settle
near the graveyard where angels sing under lampposts.

A Shawl of Spanish Moss

listen: in the rain forest behind banana trees
a sugar bird chirps

can it finally
be time for the end of grief?

dust off the coffin and sing songs
plant the moonflower atop the dirt

but don't forget: in Poland
grave no. 3 had 2000
grave no. 6 had 800
grave no. 2 had only 1

my father must be in grave no. 2

can it finally
be time for the end of grief?

don't be fooled:
grief remains distilled
and draped over the shoulders

a shawl of Spanish moss,
that fibrous lace, a boa of bones...

A Small Piece of Blotting Paper

The summer she can't stop crying
she opens an old leather case
filled with partially used
toiletries and finds a small piece
of blotting paper which holds
the handwriting of her father.

Two immortals catch her eye
from the left side of the room
and on the right, thin-boned,
white-haired women wear masks
and beaded dresses.

She anoints the edges of the pillows
and the lace antimacassars
with his cologne, the oils
of his scent. A coronation of grief.

Closing the old leather case
she puts it under her arm
and walks down the rain-slicked street,
the words of her father's letters imbedded
in the blotting paper in the box
and indelibly, under her skin.

Outside, a woman, her belly big with child,
sells blue flowers and on the train to Paris,
a man looks at a young woman's legs while
he reads Primo Levi because he knows
the dead see the dead before they die.

How a Child of Survivors Says Good-Bye

First of all, we *never* say good-bye.
It's *see you soon*. And then, whether
someone is off to the grocery store
or en route to, let's say, Paris,
we add *I love you be careful* and more
see you soons. In the time before
we were born people left thinking
they would come back but they didn't.
So, as if to cast a spell of protection,
we hug and kiss even when they
look at us and say *But I'm not going off to war!*
(What do they know?) Then—we wait,
in a fluttering kind of anxiousness,
until the door flies open, spilling bags or suitcases
and we breathe again until
the next (good-bye) *see you soon*.

Lullaby to my Father When He Finds His Mother at Long Last

We are freezing down here and the Amaryllis has broken
    ground
like a small dove trying to reach heaven.
I go to the next room and think of Saturday afternoons
when I used to boil potatoes for your lunch.
Then I ride my bicycle to Paris where on the right side
    of the street
I see the man who makes doll furniture carving a
    wooden cradle.
You would have painted it white.
Your mother is kissing you a hundred times.
I take from my pocket the last of the cake, balls of crumbs
rolling in the black cotton place. You bought me red corals
from a vendor by the sea but I think when the circus comes,
I will not wear red anymore. Did you notice?
you followed the small dove and left me here
to tend the Amaryllis. Did you notice?
your mother is kissing you a hundred times.

MIRIAM MORSEL NATHAN's poems and essays have appeared in numerous publications, including *Gargoyle, The Hampden-Sydney Poetry Review, Sojourner, The Women's Forum, the GW Forum,* and *Arts & Letters: Journal of Contemporary Culture.* Among the places she has read her work are The Knitting Factory in New York, the Smithsonian Institution, Cable TV's "Takoma Coffee House," and the U.S. Holocaust Memorial Museum. She is also director of the Washington Jewish Film Festival and was co-curator of the Israeli Film Festival for the Kennedy Center Celebration of Israel's fiftieth anniversary. Miriam and her husband live in the Washington, D.C., area and have three children.

For my late mother, Rose Brett,
and my father, Max Brett

Chapter 12

LETTING MYSELF FEEL LUCKY

Lily Brett

Lily Brett's writing is full of life. A life that was and a life that is. Beauty, in all its forms, has been a big part of both of our upbringings. I identify with everything she writes and can proudly say I have read everything she has published with great, great joy. —MW

I was thrilled to give a birth to a boy. I was ecstatic. I couldn't believe my luck. I thought our family didn't have boys. I thought they lost boys. My mother lost a son, in the Lodz ghetto. She lost four brothers, in Auschwitz, and she aborted a small boy, in shame, after the war, in Melbourne.

In Guys Hospital, in London, I couldn't sleep. I stayed up for two days and two nights looking, with amazement, at my beautiful boy. Several days later, I was even more amazed. I realized I had to take him home with me.

I hadn't thought further than giving birth to the baby I wanted. I certainly hadn't thought of taking him home. What was I thinking? I think I wasn't thinking.

I wasn't thinking about my mother. Now, I think part of the reason I had my son was my mother. I wanted to give her the sons she'd lost. I wanted to give her some of her family back. I wanted to give her the grandchildren she never dreamt she'd live to see, when she was lying, near-naked, ablaze with typhoid on the frozen ground at Stutthof, where she was sent after Auschwitz.

My baby boy made a big difference to my mother. She fell in love with him. And he fell in love with her. When she introduced him to people, she said, "My son." Sometimes, when I was there, she corrected herself, "My grandson," she would say.

Nine years ago, when she lay dying of cancer at sixty-four, she wanted him at her side. And he wanted to be there. Did I know about the fierce love that would grow between my mother and my son? The love that would fill gaps and dreams. I don't know.

I didn't know much, then. I didn't know why I got married the first time around. I married someone I'd met when I was nineteen. He was tall and blond. He was as Aryan as you could get. Later, when his blond hair darkened, I bleached it right back.

The second time I married, I was thirty-four. And I knew why I was getting married. I was crazy about him. I was crazy about a man who was a stranger. I fell in love with him minutes after I met him. What did I know? I knew something. I'm still crazy about him.

Recently, my younger daughter asked me how I could have fallen in love with someone I hardly knew. It was a hard question. I stumbled around, talking about what we unconsciously perceive and understand about each other. But she wasn't satisfied. And she was right. I didn't have an answer.

I don't have an answer to many things. I thought I would. I thought age brought answers. I think it does. But not all the answers.

I have some answers. And so I should. I've spent half my adult life in analysis. Anyone who's read my books will know the head count. Three analysts. Many years.

It has been a crucial part of my life. One that both separated me from others and gave me a greater insight into other lives, as well as my own. For most of those years, I knew no one in analysis. When I began, my mother wept and said I was casting shame over the whole family. My father said he'd heard shocking things about my analyst.

Analysis saved me. It saved me from being the least I could be. It wasn't easy. I've traveled to analysis sessions, early in the morning, four times a week, in different parts of the world. In hot weather, in below-freezing temperatures, in snowstorms, and in pouring rain. I've walked, driven, and bussed. I've cried gallons of tears. I've wept everywhere it's possible to weep. On the bus, in the car, on the streets.

But I made it. The better part of me emerged. The part of me that feels entitled to have a life. To live without paying a price. And I'm grateful. So grateful.

I'm surprised at how much gratitude I feel. I feel grateful for things I didn't notice or understand, in the past. A new sense of perspective came with the gratitude.

When I won the 1995 New South Wales Premier's Literary Award for Fiction, I said, in my acceptance speech, that my novel, *Just Like That*, was a celebration of love.

A celebration of the lives of my mother and father who survived Auschwitz. And a celebration of the fact that my mother and my father, who lost everyone they loved, in Auschwitz, did not lose the ability to love.

My mother and father survived five years in the Lodz ghetto before being transported to Auschwitz, where they were separated from each other, but not separated from their love for each other. It took them six months after the war to find each other, and they are a rare statistic—two Jewish people who were married to each other before the war, each surviving. I was very lucky to grow up in the middle of that love.

I wrote this speech very soon after being told I had won the award. I knew, and quite surprised myself by how sure I was, that it was my parents' ability to love that saved not only them after the war, but me. It took me years to see how lucky I was to experience and be the recipient of that love. I spent decades dwelling on what was missing. I spent decades wishing we weren't surrounded by the dead, by past and future Nazis, by anguish and absence.

I'm also surprised at how lucky I am able to feel. Feeling lucky has always felt dangerous. So, I've preoccupied myself with what's wrong. Once I start thinking about what's wrong, I can shuck off the discomfort that feeling lucky brings.

But, I do feel lucky. Lucky to be married to the man I'm married to. Lucky to have my children. Lucky to have lived long enough to see my children grown-up. When they were younger, I dreaded dying before they'd done enough growing. I kept detailed diaries of their childhoods, and of my feelings for them, in case I wasn't around to remind them of the past. It wasn't that I was ill. I never even caught colds, but I did catch the notion of death accompanying love. And for my parents, that was true. Everyone they were related to died, everyone they loved died.

I allowed myself to feel lucky so rarely that the moments stand out. When my son was small, he said to his best friend, within earshot of his best friend's mother, "My mother is much nicer than your mother." I was told this by the mother. When I stopped laughing, I felt very lucky to have a kid who thought that.

I feel lucky to have written the books I've written. I didn't finish high school. I threw my education away. It was only one of the valuable things I discarded. I was in the A-form, at University High School, a school for bright kids, when, seemingly out of the blue, I couldn't understand anything any teacher said. I was sixteen.

I spent the next three years trying to pass the final year of high school. I couldn't read any of the textbooks. Nothing I read made sense. Words and paragraphs swam around the page. One year I would pass French, economics, and English, the next year I would fail all three and pass something else. Another year, I gave up and went to the movies when some of the exams were held. I never managed to pass the requisite number of the right subjects in one year.

In retrospect, I realize I was having a nervous breakdown of sorts. Nobody was troubled by it at the time. My parents were bothered, and I think very puzzled, but they had greater concerns about me. I was too fat. I had to lose weight. So, this failing and flailing of a bright, young girl went largely unnoticed. No teacher commented on it.

In school photographs, I look bright and cheerful. Over the years, when I've met people I went to University High School with, they tell me they remember me, always cheerful, always laughing. What was I laughing about? Why was I looking so cheerful when I was so clearly in trouble?

I stopped trying to study, and I got a job as a journalist. Boy, was I lucky to land that job! At the job interview, no one asked me if I could write. They wanted to know if I had a car. I said, yes, a pink Valiant. I got the job. Soon, I was writing page after page of the newspaper, every week. And I hardly saw my car again.

Feeling lucky still has an edge to it. I don't want to push my luck. So, I filter and dilute my days with odd complaints and aches, and let the heady giddiness of feeling lucky seep in bits and pieces.

I'm forty-nine, now, and I can feel lucky. Physically, I've changed, too. I'm older and I'm lighter. I weigh less than I did when I was twelve, but I was a bit of a hefty twelve-year-old. I've been regaining my body, which was lost to me for years.

Feeling free is not easy for me. Still. "Freedom was never something you let yourself get away with for very long," my first analyst wrote in a letter to me fifteen years ago.

"You're much freer now," my younger daughter, who is home from college for the weekend, says to me, looking over my shoulder as I type. "You can dance, too," she says. "You never used to dance." She's right. I can dance.

"You can get out on the dance floor and have a wonderful time," she says. I smile at her.

"You're much calmer, too," she says. "It's easier to tell you when I don't like something. I don't think the world will fall apart, or anything."

I understand exactly what she's saying. She's always been a good kid. Too good. I used to worry that she felt she had to be good. That she felt I had too many demons to deal with without her adding to the distress. Last year, I bought her a T-shirt. It read, "NO MORE MS. NICE PERSON."

The former Ms. Nice Person looks at the title of this piece. "I think you've gotten older and younger," she says. "I think you take more risks than you used to. You're more curious, more confident."

This is my baby who's talking. The child, who despite the fact that she's 5'8" and in her final year of college, I can't stop feeling is still my little girl.

That was a few years ago. Now, I'm well and truly menopausal. Verified by blood tests. Jewish women, I read, statistically experience the worst menopausal symptoms. At least here, in America. And I was gearing myself up to fit right in with those statistics.

But something happened. I think it was a combination of all those years of analysis—menopause, the change of life, wasn't going to bring me any new revelations, regrets, or disturbances, not after examining every detail of every revelation and disturbance—and the walking, the weight lifting, and the eating well.

A symptomatic menopause, weight loss, dancing, biceps, and triceps. Happy endings in my own life make me nervous. I feel the need to say that this is not the perfect life. I feel the need to dredge up difficulties. I'm as imperfect as I ever was, in many ways.

And, not all the damage can be fixed up. I can't get rid of the scars of self-mutilation of my early childhood. One of them runs vertically and wildly down my stomach, the result of an unnecessary emergency appendectomy. I was only ten and wanted to cut all the excitement out of me.

I carry traces of the welts that dotted my teenage legs, red and inflamed, when I was too young to understand how distressed I was. The welts used to itch and itch. And I would scratch and scratch. I've made myself sad thinking about this. Sadness is always a good antidote for too much happiness, for me.

Some things don't change. No matter how much you think you've changed. No matter how much clarity, wisdom, maturity you may feel you've achieved. I can feel the same hurt I felt as a teenager, at a friendship not turning out to be what I imagined it was.

Friendship, deep friendship, a subject that has preoccupied me for most of my life, has, in a strange way, eluded me. I still have the occasional fantasy of the best friend. The friend who shares everything with me. The friend with whom I'm completely connected. Connected to each other, to each other's partners, to each other's children, to each other's pasts. I still long for that sometimes.

Maybe what I'm longing for is the passionate, unbridled friendship of more youthful years. Those years when you don't wait until you feel good, or look good, or it's an opportune and not inconvenient moment to call and see each other. Maybe I long for the unguarded, more truthful, less competitive friendship of the young.

A new friend, who lives in Washington, said she liked me instantly, because, as she put it to her husband, "She suffers." I can understand criteria like that.

LILY BRETT was the recipient of Australia's 1992 National Steele Rudd Award for her book, *What God Wants*. She also received the Victorian Premier's Award for poetry and is the only writer to have won Australia's highest awards for fiction and poetry. Ms. Brett was born in Germany, but moved to Melbourne with her parents in 1948. She is married to David Rankin, a prominent Australian painter, and lives in New York City.

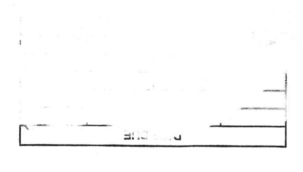